British Railways
STEAM
The Final Years
1965 - 1968

John Stretton & Peter Townsend

RAILWAY HERITAGE
from
The NOSTALGIA Collection

© John Stretton & Peter Townsend 2008
Photos: © *The* NOSTALGIA *Collection* archive / Ray Ruffell unless otherwise credited.

First published in 2008
ISBN 978 1 85794 320 7
Silver Link Publishing Ltd
The Trundle
Ringstead Road
Great Addington
Kettering
Northants NN14 4BW
Tel/Fax: 01536 330588
email: sales@nostalgiacollection.com
Website: www.nostalgiacollection.com
British Library Cataloguing in Publication Data
A catalogue record for this book is available from the British Library.
Printed and bound in The Czech Republic

Previous page **Rose Grove Shed:** The chalked messages on the smokebox door say it all! 'The End of Steam, Last Steam, The End, 2nd Aug 68' – they all leave the observer in no doubt as to the timing or relevance of the occasion. One day later than as marked, on 3 August 1968 – one of your authors' 25th birthday! – 'Black 5' 4-6-0 No 45156, once named *Ayrshire Yeomanry* but now devoid of nameplates, stands on Rose Grove shed, awaiting 'The End'. *MJS*

Above right **Waterloo:** Railwayman and photographer Ray Ruffell was no shrinking violet when it came to having his portrait captured for posterity. He delighted in chatting to engine crews and here he is at Waterloo, talking to the fireman of 'West Country' Class 4-6-2 No 34091 *Weymouth*.

Acknowledgements

As with any project, the 'headline' names are not the whole story. You will have noticed the myriads of backroom staff supporting and assisting the production of films and television shows and, though not in the same league or on the same scale, book publishing is in its way equally labyrinthine, especially on a more major project such as this one.

As well as being continually and eternally grateful to the late Ray Ruffell for pointing his camera in so many different directions and with such frequency, your authors are proud to be able to present images from his extensive collection within these pages. In addition, the following people/organisations (in no particular order) are due our thanks and gratitude: Connie Ruffell, Geoff Body, Mike Mitchell, Mike Mensing, Frank Cassell, Gary Thornton and the team at Six Bells Junction - *www.sixbellsjunction.co.uk*, The Railway Magazine, Mick Sanders, David Walshaw, Will Adams, Frances Townsend, Paul Conibeare, Colin Howard, *The West Somerset Railway*, John Leach, *The Severn Valley Railway*, Brian Morrison, John Vaughan, Michelle Littleford, Lynne Wentworth, Colin Pomeroy, Chris Ward and his ever fascinating *www.annesleyfireman.com* website, David Porter of Stafodex, Dick Manton, Mike McManus for his excellent series of books on BR Stock Changes & Withdrawal Dates. Paul Morris & Dave Cromes (for simply being just two of PT's 'best mates' over many years!). Special thanks also go to Peter Rowlands, Nic and Andrea Grant-Webb, John Garcia, Don Thompson, Michael Milward, Clive Luhrs and Brian Rose - who by calling on booksellers of all types, day in and day out -have helped you the reader, to read this book! They have **all** played their part, some with more realisation than others(!) and we are both extremely grateful to them.

With the demands of this project, not least in time, shoe-horning it between other commitments, your authors have burned much midnight oil in its preparation, but we have derived much pleasure along the way. We hope that you, the reader, will also enjoy what we have produced and, in no less a way, appreciate our time and effort in attempting to bring you an exciting, entertaining, instructive and fulfilling product.

We have endeavoured to provide a balance between the detailed perspective of the keen railway enthusiast or *gricer*, the social and industrial history enthusiast and the more general interest reader. In doing this we have tried to avoid the extensive use of mass media images in favour of the more atmospheric and 'real life' views - often taken in black & white in keeping with the majority of affordable film stock and usage of the period. There will no doubt be much 'mass media style' coverage of the last few days published elsewhere and it is our hope that our wider perspective will contribute to an overall balanced coverage for future enjoyment and of course to mark this important anniversary and thereby pay tribute to ALL railway staff past, present and future - overall in our experience a friendlier and more dedicated 'family' would be very hard to meet! Thank you one and all!

Any errors are ours entirely and we beg forgiveness if you spot any! Any corrections, comments and/or suggestions will be gladly received c/o the publisher's address. We have learned so much of the last four years of BR steam in our work on this book and we hope we may have also increased your knowledge in one or two things.

Contents

Carnforth: Another view from 3 August 1968…a different location but the same result – the end – as the moment of death is captured on film. 'Black 5' 4-6-0 No 45342 has been shunted into one of the sidings at Carnforth shed and has made its last move in service.

Still in steam, the loco was then abandoned to have its fire dropped and the term 'condemned' being applied. Externally, the front of the loco looks in good shape, an improvement to when seen on the shed four months earlier, on 15 April. *MJS*

Left **Patricroft Shed**: Among the handful of sheds that remained open to the last days of steam, there were many locomotives that were sitting idle, either with little or no work left for them to do or waiting their trip to pastures new, most often the scrap merchant's yard. One such was 'Standard' Class 5 4-6-0 No 73143, here seen enjoying the warm summer sunshine of 2 August 1968 outside Patricroft's shed building, devoid of formal shedplate or front numberplate. The hand painted replacements did nothing to enhance the loco's appearance *MJS*!

Above: One of the old school. His 'snap' bag in his hand, his work is done for the day and he is on the way home.

Left **Waterloo:** A dramatic view from the top of the Shell Building not unfortunately on the brightest of days - but with time running out for steam from this London Terminal Ray Ruffell was keen to capture the scene. An unidentified 'West Country' Class loco is seen departing with a South Coast Express. The impending change in motive power is already in evidence with an unidentified Class 50 'Warship' occupying the stabling point on the right of the approaches.

Introduction

Steam on British Railways finally came to an end officially on 4 August 1968. However, this was not the whole story, as by that time steam locomotives in day to day operations were focused in the North West of the UK. Steam in other areas of the country had been consigned to history over the previous few years.

Within the time span of this book the first region of British Railways to suffer this fate was the Western, with steam being summarily withdrawn on 31 December 1965. After that date, any ex-GWR locos at work on the erstwhile Western Region had been transferred to the Midland Region following boundary changes a year or so beforehand.

The East Coast Main Line out of King's Cross saw progressive withdrawal of steam from much earlier in the decade, but the end finally came throughout 1965 and 1966, but perhaps of more significance in the latter year was the end of steam on the Isle of Wight, the Somerset & Dorset, and Great Central Railways, with closure of those three much loved and late lamented routes. 1967 was to witness the final workings of

steam on the Southern Region and in Scotland. Steam still soldiered on in the North East of the UK to this point but was to go by the end of this year.

Thus, 1968 dawned with rapidly depleting steam services and remaining locomotives either being withdrawn or receiving basic maintenance to keep them running - often involving the use of cannibalised parts from their former glorious colleagues. In many cases, enthusiasts suddenly woke up to the impending demise of steam and began invading the North West in large numbers to witness and /or record events. There was also the sad realisation that so many once numerous and famous locomotive classes had already become extinct and this made the pilgrimage all the more important and poignant.

This book both celebrates and commemorates those last four dramatic years, recording working locomotives, shed scenes and a selected number of routes, many of which closed during the period under examination, by way of illustrating the disappearing steam age railway. The views are nostalgic, poignant and ones that cannot be repeated.

Thankfully, of course there was not to be the much feared total and final death knell for steam, thanks to the valiant efforts of hundreds of enthusiasts/volunteers who have preserved and or restored both locomotives and lines in the four decades since, with successes often far beyond what was originally envisaged.

The writing had been on the wall for many years prior to the end of BR steam in 1968, stretching back over the whole of British Railways' existence over the previous two decades and beyond. Straws in the wind had been the introduction and operation way back in 1902 of Brush & Thomson-Houston electric shunters for the NER, Nos. 26500 and 26501; Raven's 1914 design for an electric freight loco, subsequently rebuilt by the LNER in 1946 to bank on the Woodhead route; early development by GWR of the concept of diesel railcars, to save on costs of operating branch lines; Metropolitan-Vickers & Gresley designed Bo-Bo 26000 in 1941 for the LNER; Raworth & Bullied's Co-Co design for the Southern Railway, also in 1941, Nos. 20001/20002 – followed by 20003 in 1948; and LMS' work on diesel shunters in the 1930s and the introduction into traffic of 10000 and 10001 in 1947/8. Thereafter, there was a massive increase in squadron diesel shunters from the early 1950s, plus the appearance of 10100, 10800, 18000 and 18100. Steam was therefore fighting a rearguard action already by the time of the 1955 Modernisation Plan and although steam locomotives were still being built, forward planning leant towards diesels and electrics. As is well known, the last steam locomotive for BR was '9F' Class 2-10-0 No 92220 *Evening Star*, making its much-publicised exit from Swindon Works in 1960.

With line closures, changes in rail borne traffic, not least in the freight sphere, and the rapid influx of new non-steam motive power – especially in the introduction of diesel multiple units (DMUs) – on top of further changes within society that was making it progressively more difficult to recruit sufficient

Above: **Fifty years of trainspotting! Derby** – Snapped by his father, one of your authors enjoys a day out at Derby, in company with cousin David and uncle George. With 'primitive' camera around his neck, he is pleased to have portrait taken in front of 'Britannia' Class 4-6-2 No 70017 *Arrow* during the shed and Works 'Open Day' of 30 August 1958. Being 'up close and personal' to witness and savour the sheer size and majesty of these beasts was part of the attraction of the event – as well as being able to see and record the numbers of so many new and old locomotives! 92166 stands behind, taking its turn in giving access to the cab. Note the school uniform, complete with Loughborough College School badge on the blazer! Beyond, the young lad in his shorts seems a little embarrassed at having his photograph taken…where is he now? *Horace Stretton*

numbers and/or quality of staff to the railways (not least due to the sheer dirty nature of the job), it was increasingly obvious that steam had to go!

So, BR's standard gauge steam haulage died on 4 August 1968 but, despite all the wringing of hands, bemoaning the passing of an era and the doom mongers, subsequent events have proved that there is life after death!

Despite changing from 'British Railways' to 'British Rail', in a futile attempt to appear modern; the renumbering in the early 1970s of the complete diesel and electric locomotive fleet that was to continue into the future; the painting of carriage stock into the 'corporate' blue-and-grey 'image'; and the abandonment of the 'ferret and dartboard' logo in favour of the double arrow motif, our national railway system has never quite managed to finally eliminate steam from the main line!

An increasing number of steam locomotives have ventured out on to the national network in spite of, in the early years, not too well hidden attempts to throw spanners into the railtour works – the introduction of new locos onto the tracks and the proliferation of specialist railtour companies to cater for the ever-expanding enthusiast and general public touring market. Costs, debilitating last-minute cancellations and ever more restrictive requirements – many under the pretext of Health & Safety – have been hurled like grenades at the individuals and companies valiantly striving to satisfy demand but they have for the most part still survived.

2008 has seen even some of the hardest hearts softening for grand celebrations of the fortieth anniversary, even down to recreating the fabled '15 Guinea Special' of 11 August 1968; and this year should also see the emergence onto the main line by a brand new 'A1' Class, 4-6-2 No 60163 *Tornado*. 42 years since the last of the original Class was scrapped and 50 years since the last 'Peppercorn' developed locomotive was built in Darlington, this culmination of an 18 year project that many said would never succeed is a truly fitting riposte to the rumour mongers, constantly warning of costs and/or legislation being the final end for steam on the main line.

Elsewhere, these events and celebrations have been mirrored by the growing number of our private railways, who have refused to lie down under the weight of opposition, doubt and yet more legislation and have developed and expanded year

on year, even achieving re-connection to the main line in some cases. Many of the currently highly successful private lines have had their share of battles – against landowners; lack of finance; those that complained that we had reached saturation point; that there was not enough interest amongst the general public; against antipathy and some sheer bloody mindedness from authorities and local councils – but mostly all have overcome, with grit and determination, guile, innovation and, in so many cases, incredible value for money.

As with *Tornado*, the renovation of old stock has been tackled with both enthusiasm and usage of modern techniques and practices by these lines. The results are increasing attendances at Galas, special events and week by week operations of our preserved railways… and not even 'disaster', such as befell the Severn Valley Railway in the storms and floods of the Summer of 2007, can wreak total havoc. Many an organisation would have crumpled under the weight of all the negative factors – not least the repair costs of over £1m ! – but that railway's determination to be back ASAP was commendable and inspiring. As was the way that other 'sister' railways rallied round and held fund raising events. We are no longer isolated trainspotters, we are one big family, fighting against common enemies.

Who knows what time will yet bring? But one thing is certain….. While we cannot wholly and accurately recreate what was taken from us in the last years of BR steam, we can come jolly close and even improve in places. Your authors have attempted to lift the veil on the last four years of this process and we hope that you will enjoy the results of our efforts. And if you perhaps now more fully appreciate the modern day efforts to give pleasure in whatever measure to steam lovers by such as private railways and/or private locomotive owners, we shall be doubly rewarded.

Above: **Arley, Sunday 23 March 2008** 50 Years after the young John Stretton was captured on film at Derby *(See previous page)* with his uncle here we see young Alfie Russell the grandson of your other author enjoying his first visit to the Severn Valley Railway - an enthusiast in the making? Station staff at Arley are - *from left to right* - John Frank *(Booking Office)*, Ian Latimer *(Station Master)* and James Rodgers *(Porter)* - Smiles all round on this first weekend for the SVR back in service following the great storm of Summer 2007. *PT*

Left: **Closure notices** were a common sight from the mid-Fifties onwards, such as that seen at Monmouth on 4 January 1959, the last day of services. As well as advising the closure to passengers of the various stations on the route – and freight from St Briavels – locals were also notified that advance luggage facilities could be had from the replacement bus services – if they obtained tickets in advance from the few remaining open stations! *Gerald Adams/MJS collection*

BRITISH TRANSPORT COMMISSION
BRITISH RAILWAYS (WESTERN REGION)

PUBLIC NOTICE

1965

Farewell to Western Region Steam

Looking back over the past century, steam had a challenger from the earliest days. As seen in the Introduction, a straw in the wind had been the introduction way back in 1902 of Brush & Thomson-Houston electric shunters for the NER, Nos. 26500 and 26501; and around the same time, there were proposals for overhead electric traction in Snowdonia – admittedly for narrow gauge and, thus, not a direct challenge to BR – showing that steam was not to have a monopoly. Various other electric and diesel innovations came over the next half century, gathering pace by the time of Nationalisation in 1948, with LMS' work on diesel shunters in the 1930s and the introduction into traffic of 10000 and 10001 in 1947/8. The massive increase in squadron diesel shunters from the early 1950s, plus the appearance of 10100, 10800, 18000 and 18100 meant increasingly that steam was fighting a rearguard action; and the 1955 Modernisation Plan was another nail in the coffin, although steam locomotives were still being built. Social changes were also being felt by this time, with branches, stations and even some through lines coming under close scrutiny.

Between the two World Wars and continuing thereafter, railways began to face increasing competition from other modes of transport such as buses, cars, road haulage and air travel and what began as a slow trickle of closures in the 1920/30s gathered pace as the decades progressed. Dr Beeching and his infamous plan for the future survival of the railway system was not the whole cause of shrinkage in rail mileage, but certainly he did not help! The "Reshaping of British Railways" report of March 1963 proposed that out of Britain's then 18,000 miles of railway, roughly a third, some 6,000 miles (of mostly rural branch and cross-country lines) should be closed. Furthermore, many other lines should lose their passenger services and be kept open for freight only, and many of the lesser-used stations should close on lines that were to be kept open. The Conservative Government accepted the report – not really surprising in that Ernest Marples, then Transport Minister, was a director of a major

Old Oak Common: Undoubtedly there is romance and sheer aesthetic appeal with steam locomotives but, like most things, not everything is positive. The 'down side' to the steam engine was the waste material, i.e. ash and clinker. As with a domestic coal fire, this has to be regularly cleaned out or the fire will not burn. The effect of this – and the result of not clearing away equally as regularly - can readily seen here alongside 'Castle' Class 4-6-0 No 5048 *Earl of Devon*, standing alongside the detritus of many other locos on Old Oak Common shed on 4 September 1957. Wearing the 'Torbay Express' headboard, it will certainly need a clean firebox and smokebox for the run to the southwest. A long term resident of Bristol (Bath Road) shed – including when seen here – a move to South Wales came in December 1960. Finally ending up at Neath shed, withdrawal came on 11 June 1962. *D K Jones collection, MJS collection*

1968
THE END
OF STEAM
40 YEARS
2008

LCGB
3863
IX 06
82
E

Swindon Works: Over the two decades of British Railways' steam, trainspotters and enthusiasts' clubs organised trips to areas and lines that were about to lose services. Very often this was to branch lines before final closure, but other trips encompassed locations where numbers of locomotives were gathered in close proximity. One such was the LCGB's Western Ranger railtour of 15 August 1965,

seen here after arrival at Swindon Works behind '2800' Class 2-8-0 No 3863. Originating at Waterloo behind 'Standard' Class 4 4-6-0 No 75066 and ending at the same London terminus behind 'Standard' Class 4 4-6-0 No 75075, it visited Reading and Oxford as well as Swindon, plus the branches to Abingdon, Witney and Bicester (London Road). In addition to the two 'Standard 4s' and No 3863,

locos '5700' Class 0-6-0PT No 9773 and '6100' Class 2-6-2T No 6126 were also employed. As seen in the yard of Swindon Works, '2800' 2-8-0 No 3863 proudly displays 'Bristol' on the front buffer beam and the 82E shedplate that betrayed the allocation to Bristol (Barrow Road) shed. An ex-Midland Region shed, Barrow Road had been transferred to Western Region jurisdiction on 1 February 1958 and had become

nominally a diesel facility w.e.f. November 1964. No 3863 had gone there just a month before that changeover and was to serve the shed for a mere twelve months, being withdrawn less than two months after this view, on 7 October 1965.

road-building company and he believed the future lay with 'tarmac'. In addition, traffic patterns were changing, especially with freight, with large reductions in many areas of operation, not least the small factory sidings and the necessity for 'trip' workings. Thus, by the end of 1964, the need for the number of locomotives throughout the UK was rapidly diminishing, on top of increasing proliferation of non-steam motive power, with inevitable results.

During 1965, some 308 lines, branches, spurs, etc. were closed. As can be seen from the lists on pp. 20, 30 and 31, many of these were not just sleepy backwaters, but affected main lines also, such as the withdrawal of local passenger services between Bristol (Temple Meads) and Worcester; Glasgow (Central) and Carlisle; and Swindon and Bristol (Temple Meads). Others lost their passenger services completely, viz Lostwithiel to Fowey; Nuneaton to Leamington Spa (Avenue); Ruabon to Morfa Mawddach; and Carmarthen to Aberystwyth. It is self-evident from these closures alone, apart from the takeover of the diesel multiple unit (DMU) of some services prior to closure, that the number of engines required would be much reduced — and with them, the reduction in sheds to service them. The lists on pp 32 and 33 shed light (if you will excuse the pun!) on the extent of the carnage. Objections to closures and fears engendered by the proposals were recognised by Government, with the Minister of Transport announcing sample surveys of lines closing during the year — Eridge to Hailsham, Bradford to Huddersfield and Stranraer to Dumfries. Interviews with people affected before and after closure were to gauge actual hardship and the efficacy of alternative arrangements, with a view to helping future closure considerations.

It was in this year that the Western Region of BR became the first to completely eradicate steam from its metals, admittedly, with the help of transferring some previously Western sheds to the Midland Region in September 1963, such as Banbury and Wolverhampton (Oxley), although other areas such as the southern half of the ECML were progressively taking strides along the same path. As can be seen from the lists, 18 ex-GWR sheds closed completely and two — Old Oak Common and Worcester — converted to diesel operation.

Right **Westbury**: One of the 1933 introduced variants of Collett's 1929 '5700' Class 0-6-0PT, 4697 spent much of its BR life 'shuffling' along the ex-GWR main line west of Paddington, being variously allocated to Swindon (twice), Reading and Southall. A change of air was to come, however, from 24 August 1964, when a move to Exeter shed was instigated. Its stay there was not long, though, as withdrawal came on 11 July 1965. Whilst passenger duties were well within its capabilities, most of its work was as a freight engine and it is in this capacity here, at rest on Westbury shed on 23 May before returning west to Exeter. *Gerald Adams/MJS collection*

Below **Swindon Works:** When established and developed in the mid-19th century, Swindon Works was to become one of the main driving forces behind the success of the Great Western Railway. Famously, it was able to be virtually self-sufficient, manufacturing everything from nuts and bolts to completed locomotives. The steam engine was its lifeblood and, thus, the decision to end steam on the Western Region of British Railways was a body blow, coming relatively so soon after the final steam locomotive built for BR had emerged from the Works in 1960. The decline in work following the reduction of BR(WR) locos was to prove terminal twenty years later, with the complete closure of the facility. To all intents and purposes looking in fine shape, Hawksworth designed '9400' Class 0-6-0PTs Nos 8405 and 9425, seen in the Works yard on 15 August 1965, have already been withdrawn and face scrapping, less than fifteen years from new!

Above right **Ardley:** Many stations in the UK had gas lamps and some even survived right up to closure. The one at Ardley, however, south of Banbury on the former GWR main line from Birmingham to Paddington, via Bicester (North) and High Wycombe, was not quite so fortunate, where this lamp had

Others not mentioned in the list, including major facilities such as Swindon, Bristol (Bath Road) and Laira (Plymouth) had already converted to non-steam in previous years. Swindon Works had also ceased work on steam locomotives by the beginning of the year.

The year opened with British Railways announcing that it was to have a 'new face'. Out was the old name and in was 'British Rail', together with the two-way 'double arrow' that has been in prominence ever since, plus a revised typographical style, common to all Regions, on nameboards, signs, posters, timetables and for publicity purposes. The 'corporate identity' of monastral-blue and off-white livery was launched at the 'New Face of British Railways' exhibition at the Design Centre in London from 4-23 January 1965 – covering everything from tableware to uniforms to train liveries – to try to project a new image, highlight the 'improvements' since the 1955 Modernisation Plan and counter the pervading public impression that BR was not "a united, forward-looking undertaking"! A total of 66,777 people visited the exhibition,

had its gas mantle removed before passenger services ceased from 7 January 1963. When captured for posterity in June 1962, the delightful practice of station name being incorporated into the lamp

design was intact, but had now been 'enhanced' by the addition of a full but rather untidy bird's nest! *P J Garland/Roger Carpenter collection.*

Below **Swindon Works** A second view of '9400' Class 0-60PTs Nos 8405 and 9425 on 15 August. No 8405 (left) was new on the last day of 1949, going first to Banbury shed. A move to Port Talbot, in South Wales, came in August 1955 but the stay there was only for sixteen months. A move thereafter was made to Bromsgrove shed, at the foot of the Lickey Incline, on the southern outskirts of Birmingham, where it joined several of its classmates in 1956 as banker for the heavyweight freight and passenger trains climbing the steepest sustained main-line railway incline in Great Britain - two miles (3.2 km) at 1 in 37.7. Withdrawal was on 12 October 1964, by which time other forms of motive power were undertaking the banking duties. By comparison, No 9425 did not emerge from Swindon until 1951 but, like No 8405, was sent first to Banbury. Four years there ended with a move to South Wales in October 1955. A servant then of Treherbert, Cardiff (Cathays), Cardiff (Canton), Cardiff East Dock and Barry sheds, it's final home was at Aberbeeg, from where it was sidelined on 30 November 1963.

Above **Swindon Works:** Happily, not every locomotive that entered Swindon Works after withdrawal suffered from the cutter's torch.

Another view from 15 August portrays one of the lucky ones. Introduced by Collett in 1932 for light passenger work, especially on the more lightly constructed branch lines, the '6400' Class was a development of the earlier '5400s' with slightly smaller driving wheels – 4ft 7½ instead of 5ft 2 – and reduced weight, but with higher boiler pressure – 180lb compared to 165lb – and resultant greater tractive effort. They were masters of their demands and were well liked by their crews. '6400' Class 0-6-0PT No 6412, seen here, had enjoyed turns in South Wales, Devon, Cornwall and around Gloucester, from where it was deemed as surplus on 22 November 1964, exactly 30 years old and having travelled over 600,000 miles. Initially moving to the Dart Valley Railway in 1966, it was again considered surplus a decade later, when it moved to the West Somerset Railway. It can genuinely lay claim to have helped the WSR survive its early years and probably its most famous moment was when filmed on the fledgling WSR in late 1976 as the locomotive featured in the Southern TV's 'Flockton Flyer' children's programmes, complete with appropriate headboard.

Above: **Hunting Butts Tunnel**
The general rundown of ex-GWR types over the last months of steam on the BR(WR) system, caused by spreading neglect and it not being economic to lavish much in the way of attention and/or maintenance on them, led to many being in disgraceful condition. One such is 'Hall' Class 4-6-0 No 6953 *Leighton Hall*, in despicable condition without either front or cabside number plates and lacking its pride and joy, the nameplates. Converted to oil burning for a short period to November 1948, when it was renumbered as 3953, it was a London Division loco for much of its life, being an incumbent of Oxford shed from October 1950 with the exception of six months at Didcot in 1965. Presumably pressed into summer Saturday service on 14 August by Oxford shed, who had just received it back from Didcot, it is here approaching Hunting Butts Tunnel, north of Cheltenham, with the 11.22 a.m. Newquay -Wolverhampton (Low Level) holiday train. *Mike Mensing*

SPEED 4 MPH THROUGH FACING POINTS

Below: We are again at Swindon Works on 15 August, this time investigating the inhabitants of the scrap yard, 'out back' of the main Works site and in full view of the London - Bristol main line. Left to right we have: '6400' Class 0-60PT No 6412 (awaiting removal for preservation – as already seen), one of Churchward's 1903 design of 'Heavy Goods' '2800' Class 2-8-0 No 2818 – a design that proved its worth by being hard at work through to the very last years of steam on the erstwhile GWR metals, and '1400' Class 0-4-2T No 1442.

No 2818 was a resident of Swindon shed between August 1952 and September 1959; other allocations for this engine – all major, front line depots - were Bristol (St Philips Marsh), Cardiff (Canton), Newport (Ebbw Junction) and Neath where the end came on 2 November 1963. Happily No 2818 escaped the cutters torch and has made it into preservation and is part of the National Collection based at the NRM in York. Contrasting with the heavy goods locomotive, 1442 was a member of a class, introduced by Collett in 1932, built for much lighter, passenger work. Serving British Railways initially from Slough (for the Marlow branch), Reading and Oxford (twice), it decamped southwards to Westbury on 3 November 1962, before continuing the progression south and west, to various depots in Devon and Cornwall.

Withdrawal was at Laira (Plymouth) on 6 May 1965 and the loco was, therefore, a relatively recent arrival in the line here. Visitors to Tiverton Museum in Devon will be pleasantly surprised to find that dominating the Gallery is none other than No 1442 (The Tivvy Bumper). Having pulled the very last passenger train to Tiverton (Exe Valley line) in October 1964, before arriving at Swindon, she was purchased and rescued from the scrap line by the Museum Trust with a very generous grant from *Viscount Amory*. Note the enthusiasts taking advantage of the empty tender of 2818 for a panoramic view of others in the scrap yard!

We are still at Swindon Works on 15 August and again see '2800' Class 2-8-0 No 3863 on its LCGB railtour duty, but now turned and coupled up ready for the return half of the tour, due away at 2.10 p.m. The itinerary will next be: Swindon Works - Rodbourne Lane - Swindon - Foxhall Jn - Didcot North Jn – Radley, where, due at 3.06 p.m., the 2-8-0 will uncouple, for the run down the branch to Abingdon – and then on through Oxford to the Witney Branch – comprising just three of the coaches, to be handled by '5700' Class 0-6-0PT No 9773. Another of the 1933 variant of the Collett 1929 design – see No 4697 on *page 8* – No 9773 was an extremely 'loyal' servant, having

breaking previous records at the Centre. Alongside this, the 24-hr clock was being introduced throughout the system, following its first appearance at Glasgow, St Enoch Station during the summer of 1964; and the first Station Managers, as opposed to stationmasters, were appointed at Paddington, Euston and St Pancras.

Other events so soon after New Year's Day saw steam eliminated from the Reading-Tonbridge line; Rugby replace Nuneaton as the changeover point for locomotives, as the WCML electrification spread south from Crewe; the traffic chief of ICI publicly stating that the failure of rail transport to meet the needs of industry has led to growth in private hauliers; fare increases were made from 1 February – by ¼d a mile in ordinary second-class fares (from 3d to 3¼d) and 5% on first class; severe flooding in December 1964 saw extensive damage between Llangollen Goods Junction and Bala Junction and the premature end of the section by January 18; announcement of withdrawal of passenger services from Bournemouth West during the summer – actually on 2 August; Tom Fraser, Minister of Transport, refused permission to end passenger services between Glasgow and Edinburgh, via Shotts; Darlington - Richmond; and Carlisle to Hellifield. In hindsight, these were wise decisions, but he did agree, among others, to close 13 stations on the Shrewsbury-Aberystwyth route and the line service from Halwill to Torrington; and to allow BR Works to tender for outside work. The 'Mark II' first-class corridor coaches were under construction at Derby Works; and a new 10-year contract was signed to transport GPO parcels! It was also announced that Dr Beeching would leave the BRB and return to ICI in June; and, on 30 January, Sir Winston Churchill's funeral train was hauled from Waterloo to Handborough, on the Oxford-Worcester line, by 'Battle of Britain' Class 4-6-2 No 34051 *Winston Churchill.*

only two homes in British Railways days. A Swindon shed resident prior to and at Nationalisation in 1948, it stayed there until 6 November 1964, whence it transferred allegiance to Oxford. This place

of work was to be short-lived, however, with the end coming with the summary dismissal of steam on BR(WR) on 31 December 1965. Official withdrawal date was 15 January 1966.

The period to 8 January saw no fewer than 92 WR-based steam locomotives withdrawn, including 12 'Halls', 3 'Castles', 3 'Granges', 4 'Manors', 2 Stanier '8Fs' and 7 'Standards'; and gas turbine locomotive 18000 was returned to Switzerland; but Brush prototype Type 4 D0280 *Falcon* was delivered to the WR; preserved 'A3' *Flying Scotsman* had a general repair and overhaul at Darlington; and a new named train – 'The Hebridean', running between Inverness and Kyle of Lochalsh – was introduced on 25 January. Elsewhere, a further stretch of the ECML was upgraded to 100 mph running, between Cadwell, north of Hitchin and a point south of Offord; a rail-road air-link service was introduced from Slough station to London Airport; a 'Western Weekender' ticket was issued on certain journeys on the WR, at reduced fare rates; a disused one-mile section of the Headfield branch was relaid by BR(NER) to serve the goods depot and coal concentration yard at Dewsbury Railway Street; and a second public auction of railway relics and equipment was held at Derby.

During the summer, a new service was introduced by BR(WR), offering BR's cheapest deal for the family motorist. Running from Kensington Olympia station to Fishguard, the 'London-Irish Car Carrier' service linked with the drive-on-drive-off ferry to Rosslare, with weekend facilities beginning on June 18 and weekdays from 11 July to 25 September.

1968 THE END OF STEAM 2008

Below: **Hunting Butts Tunnel** Swinging through 180° from the picture on *page 14*, 'Hall' Class 4-6-0 No 6953 *Leighton Hall* is seen again, this time on the final approach to the 97-yard Hunting Butts Tunnel, which can be seen ahead of the train. The grimy and unkempt nature of the loco is mirrored by the smoke, which, by the colour, is either a result of the loco's condition or from some mishandling of the coaling by the fireman. The far side of the tunnel is within sight of Cheltenham Racecourse station, now restored to operations by the private Gloucestershire Warwickshire Railway. To those of us old enough to remember them, this view of the maroon corridor coaches brings back happy memories. *Mike Mensing*

PLATFORM 1

Left **Reading General** Despite a majority of photographs being bog-standard front-three-quarter views, head-on portraits of steam locomotives can be powerful images, especially when the present of steam is self-evident, as here. On 4 April 1965, 'Modified Hall' Class 4-6-0 No 6963 *Throwley Hall* stands at Reading General station at the head of LCGB's The Wessex Downsman Railtour. The trip had begun at Waterloo at 9.18 a.m. behind 'S15' Class 4-6-0 No 30837, reaching Reading at 11.10, some nine minutes late after a longer than scheduled stop at Ascot. Further time was lost with the change of locos at Reading and eventual departure was 18 minutes down!

Despite not bearing a shedplate on this day, No 6963 was an incumbent of Reading shed and had been since 4 May 1964, surviving a brief period of withdrawal before being reinstated on 27 December of that year. It was a much travelled loco, having been allocated at various sheds in the West Midlands and South Wales before its move to Reading and, then going on to serve both Didcot and Oxford before the final curtain at the latter shed on 8 August 1965.

GENTLEMEN

Leaving London at 11.55 p.m., cars and passengers were to be in Ireland by 10.15 the next morning and, with a capacity of 28 cars per train of open flat-deck vehicles, the intention was to develop a new market and counter growing congestion on the roads! Authorisation was given for a new diesel servicing depot at Severn Tunnel Junction, to replace the steam shed, with work to start in September; and by this time, there were over 100 locomotives at Dai Woodham's Barry scrapyard including 15 Bullied Pacifics. Locomotives were also cut up at Banbury shed for the first time. Slightly earlier in the year, following protests from passengers over the riding of the suburban DMU stock introduced on the Manchester-North Wales service, steam was brought back onto the trains w.e.f. 22 March. Sadly, however, this change was only temporary, being a stopgap until inter-city type DMUs could be introduced. Steam was also brought back into action in Scotland, following blizzards in the southwest on 3 March, as the DMUs were not able to cope with the snowdrifts! For services to Stranraer, this lasted for five days.

A precursor of what would turn out to be a more major development on the ground, was the announcement of a 'remodelling of track and platforms', to allow Reading General station to accept trains that had formerly run into the Southern station. This was intended to both cut day-to-day running costs in the area and release 12 acres of railway land for redevelopment; and was an almost direct result of the transfer of the Southern station to BR(WR) jurisdiction earlier in the year. Other nails in steam's coffin, was the 7th International Congress on Combustion Engines, held in Marylebone Goods Yard from 25-29 April, with BR keen to show technical advances in diesel traction over the previous decade; and 11 June seeing the last regularly scheduled steam-hauled service – the 1615 to Banbury – leave Paddington, behind 'Castle' Class 4-6-0 No 7029 *Clun Castle*.

June also saw another momentous event. On the 5th, the heaviest single load ever carried by British Railways was a 240-ton boiler drum, measuring 122ft long and with a 6ft circumference, resting on cradles placed on two 12-wheeled bogies. It made the 108-mile journey from Ettingshall Road Goods Station in Wolverhampton over a specially surveyed route, through Walsall, Lichfield, Burton-on-Trent, Derby, Trent, Clay Cross and Chesterfield on its way to the CEGB's Eggborough Power Station, near Goole. Speeds were between 5 and 20 mph, with the consist leaving Wolverhampton at 12.37.

Left: Even as late as 1965 there were many fascinating items of historical interest dating back to the pre nationalised railways. Here a sign at Lydney Junction, on the erstwhile Severn & Wye Joint Railway, proudly proclaims:

**Great Western
& Midland Railways**

All persons are warned not to trespass upon the railway or upon any station thereon and notice is hereby given that pursuant to provisions of the Companies' Acts every person who trespasses upon this railway or upon any station thereon in such a manner as to expose himself to danger or risk of danger renders himself liable to a penalty of forty shillings and in default of payment to one months imprisonment for every such offence.
By Order

One wonders if 'herself' would be similarly treated?

Below **Patney & Chirton:** Leaving Reading, the tour had taken the line through Newbury and Bedwyn before pausing for a 'photo-stop' at Patney & Chirton station. It is seen here at that venue, with bodies at every conceivable vantage point, with an unidentified 'Hymek' diesel passing light engine on the up line. The ten minutes stop here was scheduled, but the tour was now 48 minutes late…. and worse was to come! No 6963 took the train onto Bristol (Temple Meads) station, which was reached 51 minutes down and yet more time being lost with another change of motive power. Subsequently travelling over the Somerset & Dorset route to Bournemouth, the return to Waterloo was by the BR(SR) main line. Sadly, yet more time was lost on this stretch and the London end was finally achieved at 8.48 p.m. – one hour and twenty three minutes behind schedule!

Oxford Shed: One of the delights and appeals of our railway system in steam days was the engine shed, where a collection of locomotives could be seen in greater numbers in a short time than sitting by the lineside. Walking round the depots took time to record all the numbers, but when passing such a site by train, the excitement and anticipation was honed by the speed of passage and the inability to capture everything. And, surely, that unknown loco lurking just out view was just the one you needed to see!

Some appreciation of the task of recording the numbers from onboard a train can be judged from this view of Oxford shed on 13 April 1965, photographed from the 6.52 a.m. Paddington-Birmingham (Snow Hill) DMU express service. On view are (unidentified!) 'Halls', '9Fs', 'Pannier Tanks' and, although not readily apparent, the photographer records that ex-LMS and 'Standard' 'Class 5s' were also present. It is hard to realise that steam will be banished from the site at the end of the year!

Western Region

1965 LINE CLOSURES

Date	From	To	Passenger/Goods
4 January	Bristol TM	Worcester SH	*Local Passenger*
	Lostwithiel	Fowey	*Passenger*
	Swindon	Bristol TM	*Local Passenger*
18 January	Ruabon	Morfa Mawddach	*Passenger*
	Bala Jct	Bala	*Closed*
	Ellesmere	Oswestry	*Closed*
22 February	Carmarthen	Aberystwyth	*Passenger*
1 March	Torrington	Halwill	*Closed*
29 March	West Drayton	Staines W	*Passenger*
10 April	Bewdley	Cleobury Mortimer	*Closed*
20 September	Chippenham	Calne	*Closed*
4 October	Kemble	Cirencester Town	*Closed*
	Barnstaple Jnct	Torrington	*Passenger*
1 November	Grange Court	Ross on Wye	*Closed*
	Ross on Wye	Lydbrook Jnct	*Closed*

Please note: The colours represent the BR Region in which the shed was allocated. Previous (in Date column) and subsequent (in non Date column) changes to the sheds Regional allocation are reflected by the mix colours on a row or rows

As the summer progressed, work began on the Glasgow-Wemyss Bay electrification; the Southern Region scrapped a bundle of cheap fares and introduced a standard cheap-day return fare based on mileage; the North London passenger services between Richmond and Broad Street were reprieved from withdrawal; Blackpool Corporation sanctioned plans to turn Central Station into a bingo hall!; the Bluebell Railway Preservation Society celebrated five years of operations; preserved 'Princess' Class 4-6-2 No 46201 *Princess Elizabeth* was steamed for the first time in private hands, at Ashchurch; The Severn Valley Railway Society was born; and another huge swathe was cut through the numbers of ex-GWR locomotives in service. Meanwhile, a new diesel depot was opened at Shirebrook West, with full maintenance facilities, including sandbox towers, capable of handling 30 mainline locomotives and 19 350-hp shunters and laying the grounds for the closure to steam of Langwith Junction shed in February 1966. In Scotland, Edinburgh Princes Street station closed on 6 September; and it was announced that Glasgow St Enoch station would close during 1966; whilst in Wales, the magnificent Crumlin Viaduct was demolished, with much interest as to whether a fabled casket of new coins had been placed under one of the piers in 1853!; and not far away, Lydbrook Viaduct on the ex-S&WR was taken down. 27 September saw the death of Sir William Stanier, a Swindon-trained man who transformed the style and fortunes of LMS motive power.

Health & Safety regulations were very different in 1965, but there was sufficient concern on the Midland Region that the first high visibility clothing was introduced on the WCML, in an attempt to reduce accidents among rail workers.

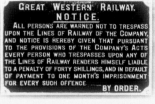

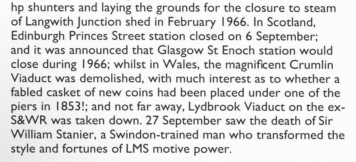

Below **Branksome:** While large sheds gave greater numbers, smaller facilities could provide equal pleasure in quiet corners. One such was Branksome, in Dorset, one of the sub-sheds of Bournemouth. Situated east of Branksome station, in the fork of lines to Bournemouth West and Central stations, it was built by the Somerset & Dorset Joint Railway and opened in 1895. A two-road straight shed, it was closed temporarily by the LMS as a wartime measure but reopened sometime after hostilities had ended. BR removed the turntable and the corrugated iron structure was replaced by asbestos sheeting before closure came on 2 August 1965. Just a few months before this, on 10 March, '2251' Class 0-6-0 No 3218 is captured on shed between duties, having arrived by way of a freight from Templecombe. Looking highly respectable and in good external condition, complete with cabside numberplate and route availability marking, 'ferret and dartboard' BR logo and cab protective tarpaulin draped over the roof, the loco has only a further three months of life, being withdrawn on 13 June. Allocated to Templecombe shed when seen here, it had previously worked out of Banbury (when new in March 1948), Stourbridge, Worcester and two of the three sheds in Bristol.

Below **Haresfield:** Seemingly, towards the end, shedmasters did not care about the external condition of the locos they rostered for various duties – especially freight – as long as they thought they could do the job! On BR(WR), especially, ex-GWR locos so often appeared devoid of apparent signs of their true identities. On 31 July 1965, 'Hall' Class 4-6-0 No 6916 *Misterton Hall* seems in no hurry as it trundles south on the ex-GWR metals at Haresfield, with its decidedly mixed rake of wagons and produce. A crude attempt at front number is painted on the smokebox but, elsewhere, nameplates and numberplate have been removed and even the tender seems to be devoid of logo! Hereford and Shrewsbury were long time homes for the 'Hall', before a move to Banbury on 20 June 1964 (by then a BR(MR) depot). Withdrawal was, perhaps not surprisingly, less than two months after this view, on 19 September. *Gerald Adams/MJS collection*

Above **Leamington Spa:** Another of the smaller sheds that paid dividends for the visiting enthusiast was Leamington Spa. With the station being on an important inter-urban and cross-country route, one never quite knew what might be lurking within the shed boundaries. Late in its life, on 13 April 1965, as seen from a passing Inter-City express, an ex-GWR 2-6-2T and WD 'Austerity' 2-8-0 grace the yard. Situated on the east side of the line, some distance south of the General station, this facility was opened by the GWR in September 1906, to replace the earlier shed – to the north of the line west of the station – which had been destroyed by fire in 1902. The newer shed had four roads, a ramped coaling stage, water tower and turntable. It was closed two months after this view, on 14 June, demolished and the site buried under an industrial estate.

Devizes: In the heady days of railtours in the 1950s/60s, when, seemingly, trains went everywhere that the enthusiasts wished and requested motive power was as often as not provided, it was not unusual to see tour participants wandering all over the place during stops, whether as photo shoots or to change engines. We have already seen 'Hall' Class 4-6-0 No 6963 *Throwley Hall* at the head of LCGB's The Wessex Downsman on 4 April (see p.16) but here we again see it a month later, on 2 May, on a virtual recreation of the first tour, with the same title, visiting most of the same places and with most of the same motive power in use. On this later date, the tour has paused at Devizes to give members a ten minute opportunity to stretch their legs – well and truly in this picture! – and take their photographs. Now into the early years of the 'Swinging Sixties', there are signs of a shift in outlook and fashions. Whereas ten years previously, tours would have been the preserve of (predominantly) males in suits and ties, there are now a few ladies appearing and more casual dress is percolating the male population – though still with shirts and ties under the casual jackets!

Tinsley marshalling yard was opened on 29 October; the same month that Old Oak Common diesel depot was opened to replace the erstwhile 81A steam shed; the last stretch to complete the Liverpool-Euston WCML electrification was energised on 25th; and that saw BR undertake week long surveys of passengers views in the southwest and northeast.

The year ended with cash registers being installed in ticket offices of the SR!; and the appointment of Barbara Castle as the country's first female Minister of Transport.

1968
THE END
OF STEAM
2008

A Selection of 1965 Station Closures (all Regions)

4 January	Law Junction, Symington, Abington, Elvanfoot, Wootton Bassett, Corsham, Box, Bathford
1 February	Glasgow Eglington Street,
1 March	Watergate, Petrockstow, Meeth, Hatherleigh, Hole
8 March	Cloughton, Ravenscar, Robin Hood's Bay, Goathland, Levisham, Pickering, Crook
22 March	Kirkstall, Apperley Bridge, Manningham, Saltaire, Embsay, Bolton Abbey
29 March	Colnbrook, Staines West
26 April	Wheathampstead, Harpenden East, Luton Hoo and Bute Street, Dunstable Town and North
14 June	Low Moor, Cleckheaton, Heckmondwike, Liversedge, Castle Douglas, Gatehouse of Fleet, Newton Stewart, Castle Kennedy, Forden, Montgomery, Abermule, Carno, Talerddig, Cemmes Road, Ynyslas
28 June	Bromford Bridge
6 September	Edinburgh Princes Street, Kilkerran, Glenwhilly
13 September	Haigh, Crigglestone, Ferrybridge, Bolton Percy
20 September	Calne
1 November	Gateshead West, Tollerton, Leadenham, Langworth, North Kelsey
29 November	Earswick, Pocklington, Market Weighton
6 December	Auchinleck, Cumnock, Sanquhar, Gretna Green

Left **Reading:** It was inevitable, with the rapidly approaching disappearance of steam on ex-GWR/ BR(WR) metals, that special tours using appropriate motive power would be numerous and very popular during 1965. Whilst other areas of the UK were not ignored, a fair proportion of the year's railtours concentrated on the South. There was a two-day RCTS/SLS joint extravaganza over the weekend of 25/26 September, as the Farewell to Steam in West Wales Railtour, which explored branch lines from Swansea on the Saturday and the main line west from Swansea on the Sunday, but there was to be a later valedictory special, on 20 November. Rather grandly titled 'Paddington Steam Farewell Railtour', the LCGB employed popular 'Castle' Class 4-6-0 No 4079 *Pendennis Castle* to haul 'a grand day out' from Paddington to Oxford, Worcester, Cheltenham, Gloucester and Swindon, before a fast run back to the metropolis.

With the special headcode 'Z40', the outward train is seen from the remains of the West Main signalbox, accelerating out of Reading in less than ideal weather conditions. Named after a castle in Cornwall, the loco had already been withdrawn for over a year when photographed, but had been retained for preservation, partly celebrating its part in the LNER trials in April 1925, proving the worth of GWR design along the ECML out of King's Cross (with Driver Young and Fireman Pearce in charge). Originally built at Swindon in 1924, subsequent history saw it travel to Australia courtesy of the Hammerseley Iron Co. Following a return to the UK, No 4079 is now under the care of the GWS, for restoration at Didcot, smaller items of the loco arrived on site in Oxfordshire in May 2000, to be followed by the main loco and a press call in July.

Below **Kingham:** Another picture, taken on 12 May 1965, of the disgustingly dishevelled condition so prevalent in the last months of GWR steam. 'Manor' Class 4-6-0 No 7804 *Baydon Manor* stands in Kingham station, still with cab numberplate but without the equivalent on the smokebox front or nameplate. The photographer has not recorded the working but with the signal at the far end of the platform apparently giving the road for the sidings left of the main line, it is quite possible that the 'Manor' is indulging in a little shunting, or, perhaps, is on engineering duties and is about to clear the line. Certainly, with the brakevan next to it, it is unlikely to be heading off down the main line towards Worcester and it is to be hoped that mechanically it was in far better condition than that on view! New in the last years before WWII,

No 7804 spent much of its early life in Devon but was catapulted northwest in June 1954 into the rigours of working in South Wales. The first allocation in the Principality was to Carmarthen, for the 'Cambrian Coast Express' workings up to Aberystwyth and beyond. More menial tasks were allotted eight years later, with a move to the predominantly freight shed at Llanelli – its home shed when seen here in Oxfordshire! – followed by a very short life for just one month at Severn Tunnel Junction between August and September 1965.
Gerald Adams/MJS collection

Left **Chipping Norton:** ….and not a drop to drink! An amusing pose and a poignant portrait of a much-loved station summarily abandoned. The scene is Chipping Norton on 12 May 1965, nine months after final closure with the withdrawal of passenger services. Freight had been ended two years earlier. Abandoned is the apposite word for the devastation wrought by the demolition gang and the detritus they have left behind. Water still drips lazily from the 'bag', but pulling the chain will not create any more cascades at this location. All the track has gone, but the point rodding still runs alongside the far platform, leading to the signals still in situ by the A44 road overbridge; sleepers 'snooze' along the platform surface; the footbridge is still in situ; and the station nameboard struggles, left, to avoid the clutches of the undergrowth! *Gerald Adams/ MJS collection*

Right **Radley:** In contrast to Chipping Norton, this scene is from a station that remains open for business into the 21st century, albeit much changed!
On 17 July 1965, 'Hall' Class 4-6-0 No 7919 *Runter Hall* bursts under the covered footbridge at Radley with a semi-fast service, next stop Oxford. Once a junction station for the Abingdon branch – the bay platform for which was out of sight to the right of this view – this status ceased with the ending of services to the town on 9 September 1963. In 2008, the footbridge still serves to cross the line but now without canopy; and the station is also bereft of shelter, with passengers having to take their chances with the weather! No 7919 was new to Reading shed on 31 May 1950, one of several locomotives that continued to be built at Swindon in British Railways' days but to a GWR design! It stayed at that shed until 10 Janaury 1965, after which it moved to Oxford on 11 July (six days before this view) and survived to the very end of steam on the GWR. Its official withdrawal date was 16 January 1966 and it was scrapped at Cashmore's, Newport. *Gerald Adams/MJS collection*

Rail tours by enthusiast groups had been popular for many a long year, indeed from the earliest days of the interest engendered by the railways amongst non railway workers. With the closure of so many branch lines and the inexhorable decline in steam motive power the number of tours and their popularity was growing at a pace...

The rail tour list for 1965 as reported on the popular *Six Bells Junction* web site was at the time of writing as follows:

Date	Railtour Operator	Tour name
31/12/65	BR (NER)	???
27/12/65	BR	(Football Special)
12/12/65	LCGB	Cross Countryman
11/12/65	WRS	Waverley Railtour
05/12/65	LCGB	Steyning Line Railtour
04/12/65	RCTS	Jubilee Commemorative Rail Tour
04/12/65	BR	(Football Special)
27/11/65	WRS	Midlander Railtour
27/11/65	BR	Last Steam Hauled Train from Paddington
20/11/65	LCGB	Paddington Steam Farewell Railtour
13/11/65	WRS	Yorkshireman No1
13/11/65	???	Panda Pullman
06/11/65	LCGB	Border Counties Railtour
23/10/65	RCTS	South Yorkshire No5 Rail Tour
23/10/65	A4PS	???
17/10/65	LCGB	Derbyshire Railtour
17/10/65	BLS	???
17/10/65	SLS	???

Date	Railtour Operator	Tour name
16/10/65	RCTS	Midlands Locomotive Requiem Rail Tour
16/10/65	BLS	???
03/10/65	SCTS	Exeter Flyer
03/10/65	LCGB	Vectis Farewell Railtour
03/10/65	L&WRPS	(Wissington Light Railway)
02/10/65	RCTS	North Lincolnshire Rail Tour
26/09/65	RCTS/SLS	Farewell to Steam in West Wales Railtour
25/09/65	RCTS/SLS	Farewell to Steam in West Wales Railtour
25/09/65	LCGB	Glazier Brakevan Tour
25/09/65	Ian Allan	(Talyllyn Railway AGM)
19/09/65	RCTS	Blyth & Tyne Rail Tour
19/09/65	SLS	Restored Locomotives Cavalcade
18/09/65	LCGB	High Peak Railtour
12/09/65	SCTS	Exeter Flyer
12/09/65	GMRS	???
11/09/65	SLS/MLS	Shropshire Railtour

Continues overleaf

Lost lines around the other regions

London Midland Region
Eastern Region
North Eastern Region
Scottish Region
Southern Region

Date	Railtour Operator	Tour name
05/09/65	WRS	Hants & Dorset Rail Tour
05/09/65	GWS	Launceston Branch Centenary Tour 1865 - 1965
05/09/65	HR	South Yorkshireman
04/09/65	LNER	LNER Pacific Tour
04/09/65	WRS	Pennine Tour
30/08/65	?BR?	???
29/08/65	BR	(Anglers' Excursion)
28/08/65	RCTS	Fife Coast Tour
27/08/65	BR	???
26/08/65	BR	???
25/08/65	BR	???
24/08/65	BR	???
21/08/65	?BR?	???
15/08/65	LCGB	Western Ranger
15/08/65	???	???
08/08/65	Ian Allan	???
07/08/65	LCGB	Middleton Branch Brakevan Tour
01/08/65	WRS	Ten Counties
31/07/65	SRC	Rambling 56
25/07/65	LCGB/REC	Thames Valley Railtour
11/07/65	PRC	Diesel Rail Tour
04/07/65	RRWMC	(Day Excursion)
03/07/65	LCGB	Northampton Branches Brake Van Railtour
13/06/65	LCGB	Wealdsman
12/06/65	REC	???
12/06/65	WRS	Somerset & Dorset Joint & Eastleigh Tour
07/06/65	???	???
05/06/65	SLPF	???
30/05/65	LCGB	Pas de Calais Railtour
30/05/65	HCRS	Isle of Wight
29/05/65	RCTS	East Midlander No 8
29/05/65	NLWMC	(Day Excursion)

1965 LINE CLOSURES

Date	From	To	Passenger/Goods
4 January	Leek	Uttoxeter	Passenger
18 January	Birmingham NS	Walsall	Passenger
	Nuneaton	Leamington Spa	Passenger
	Walsall	Rugeley TV	Passenger
	Wolverhampton HL	Burton on Trent	Passenger
6 September	Nottingham	Kirkby-in-Ashfield	Passenger
14 June	Eridge	Hailsham	Passenger
	Christ's Hospital	Guildford	Closed
2 August	Bournemouth C	Bournemouth West	Passenger
	Branksome	Bournemouth West	Closed
29 November	Lyme Regis	Axminster	Closed
8 March	Bishop Auckland	Crook	Passenger
	Sheffield Victoria	York	Passenger
	Pickering	Grosmont	Closed
	Scarborough	Whitby	Closed
22 March	Leeds City	Bradford Forster Sq.	Local Passenger
	Ilkley	Skipton	Closed
29 March	Tweedmouth	Kelso	Closed
3 May	Sunderland	South Shields	Passenger
14 June	Bradford Exch.	Huddersfield	Passenger
29 November	Hull	York (via Beverley)	Passenger
4 January	Glasgow Central	Carlisle	Local Passenger
29 March	Tweedmouth	Kelso	Closed
3 May	Aberdeen	Peterhead	Passenger
	Inverness	Perth	Local Passenger
14 June	Dumfries	Stranraer	Passenger
6 August	Ayr	Stranraer	Local Passenger
6 December	Glasgow St En.	Carlisle (via Kilmarnock)	Local Passenger

1965 LINE CLOSURES

Date	From	To	Passenger/ Goods
8 March	Swinton Town	Mexborough	*Closed*
1 April	Bawtry	Misson	*Closed*
13 September	Newmarket	Fordham	*Closed*
20 September	St. Margarets	Buntingford	*Closed*
1 November	Grantham	Lincoln City	*Passenger*
	Lincoln	Barnetby	*Local Passenger*

Date	Railtour Operator	Tour name
23/05/65	WRST	Merchant Navy Locomotive Tour to Swindon & Eastleigh
23/05/65	SLS	Bullied Pacific Rail Tour
22/05/65	RCTS	Cheshire Lines Centenarian Railtour
22/05/65	BR	(Territorial Army Special)
15/05/65	SLS	(Brake Van Tour)
09/05/65	???	???
08/05/65	LUPTS	Mersey Docks Rail Tour
08/05/65	WRS	South Yorks & Notts Railtour
08/05/65	BR	(Troop Train)
02/05/65	LCGB	Wessex Downsman
01/05/65	FRS	???
01/05/65	?BR?	(Football Special)
24/04/65	LCGB	Notts & Lincs Railtour
24/04/65	SLS	Farewell to the Stratford-upon-Avon and Midland Junction Railway Tour
21/04/65	Ian Allan	???
19/04/65	BLS	Scottish Rambler No4 Railtour
18/04/65	BLS	Scottish Rambler No4 Railtour
17/04/65	BLS	Scottish Rambler No4 Railtour
16/04/65	BLS	Scottish Rambler No4 Brake Van Tour
10/04/65	RCTS	North Eastern No2 Railtour
10/04/65	RECF	Bosworth
04/04/65	LCGB	Wessex Downsman
28/03/65	SCTS	Southern Wanderer
27/03/65	PRC/RCTS	Exmoor Ranger
27/03/65	S&WRS	???
27/03/65	Ian Allan	Lickey & Midlands Railtour
27/03/65	???	(Football Special)
26/03/65	CGS	(School Special)
21/03/65	RCTS	Tyne-Solway Rail Tour
20/03/65	LCGB	Bristol Flyer
13/03/65	BR	(Rugby Union Special)
13/03/65	CGS	(School Special)

Date	Railtour Operator	Tour name
13/03/65	MURS	Staffordshire Potter Railtour
07/03/65	LCGB	East Devon
07/03/65	HCRS	Six Counties
06/03/65	SLS/MLS	Whitby Moors Railtour
28/02/65	LCGB	East Devon
20/02/65	BR	(Football Specials)
13/02/65	RCTS	Rebuilt Scot Commemorative Rail Tour
06/02-07/02/65	BR	(Rugby Specials)
06/02/65	LCGB	Western Venturer
??/02/65	BR	(Football Special)
30/01/65	BR	(Football Specials)
30/01/65	BR	(Football Special)
30/01/65	BR	(Football Special)
30/01/65	BR	(?Football or Day? Excursion)
24/01/65	SLS	Farewell To The Castles
17/01/65	SLS	Cambrian Tour
16/01/65	BR	(Rugby Specials)
11/01/65	???	???
09/01/65	BR	(Football Specials) - 2 trains
09/01/65	BR	(Football Specials) - 3 trains
03/01/65	LCGB	Maunsell Commemorative

The Lion & Wheel logo appeared in many forms over the British Railways years from 1948 - 1965. The version shown above was applied to locomotives between 1948 and 1956 but as with any semi-permanent livery was still to be seen on locomotives and tenders for some considerable time after the replacement logo was introduced, The logo above was also affectionately (?) known as the Ferret and Dartboard logo for reasons that are to your author's view far from clear - the dartboard reference is obvious but the lion in our view is as far from a ferret as the jungle is to the farm yard! *PT*

Left: **Minehead** The lion and wheel logo as described above is seen here in use on preserved '5205' Class 2-8-0T No 5224 and the sole surviving 'Super D' Class G2 0-8-0 No 49395 seen at the West Somerset Steam Railway gala on 14 March 2008. *MJS*

Locoshed closures by region

London Midland Region
Eastern Region
North Eastern Region
Scottish Region
Southern Region
Western Region

1965 SHED CLOSURES

Date	Code	Name	Steam/Closed
27 August	1A	Willesden	Closed
29 March	1C	Watford	Closed
15 July	1E	Bletchley	Closed
25 May	2A	Rugby	Steam
27 September	2E	Northampton	Closed
14 June	2F	Woodford Halse	Closed
24 May	5A	Crewe North	Closed
19 July	5C	Stafford	Closed
14 June	6A	Bangor	Closed

14 February	9A	Longsight	Steam
14 June	9G	Gorton	Closed
14 June	15B	Kettering	Closed
4 October	15D	Coalville	Closed
4 October	15F	Market Harborough	Closed
4 April	16A	Nottingham	Closed
? December	18A	Toton	Steam
12 April	21C	Bushbury	Closed
11 October	21D	Aston	Closed
12 November	26D	Bury	Closed
3 January	34E	New England	Steam
14 June	36E	Retford	Closed
11 October	41D	Canklow	Closed
4 October	41E	Barrow Hill	Steam
14 June	41H	Staveley (GC)	Closed
20 March	52A	Gateshead	Steam
24 August	52K	Consett	Closed
? October	56B	Ardsley	Closed
3 October	64C	Dalrey Road	Closed
18 October	65C	Parkhead	Closed
12 October	65F	Grangemouth	Steam
? February	67D	Ardrossan	Steam
? June	72A	Exmouth Junction	Steam
? June	72C	Yeovil Town	Closed
4 January	75B	Redhill	Closed
22 March	81A	Old Oak Common	Steam
4 January	81D	Reading	Closed
29 May	81E	Didcot	Closed

Below **Cardiff East Dock:** Line closures, both before and after Beeching, left a legacy of reduction in the need for steam locomotives. The advent of dieselisation, both in terms of locos and multiple units, added weight to the abandonment of whole classes of engines, often including those that had only been built, at great cost, a matter of a handful of years previously. Shed closures followed and the conjunction of all these influences was the mass accumulation of locos at many points throughout the 1960s and across the country. A case in point is seen here in this view of Cardiff East Dock shed on 4 June 1965, where at least 27 ex-GWR tanks (and there are no tender engines in view) are gathered awaiting their grim fate. Closest to the camera are '5101' Class 2-8-0 No 4169, '5700' Class 0-60PT No 9651, '7200' Class 2-8-2T No 7210 and '4200' Class 2-8-0T No 4285. They were withdrawn, respectively, on 13 June, and 16 May (last three). No 4169, new on 30 November 1948, spent the whole of its life

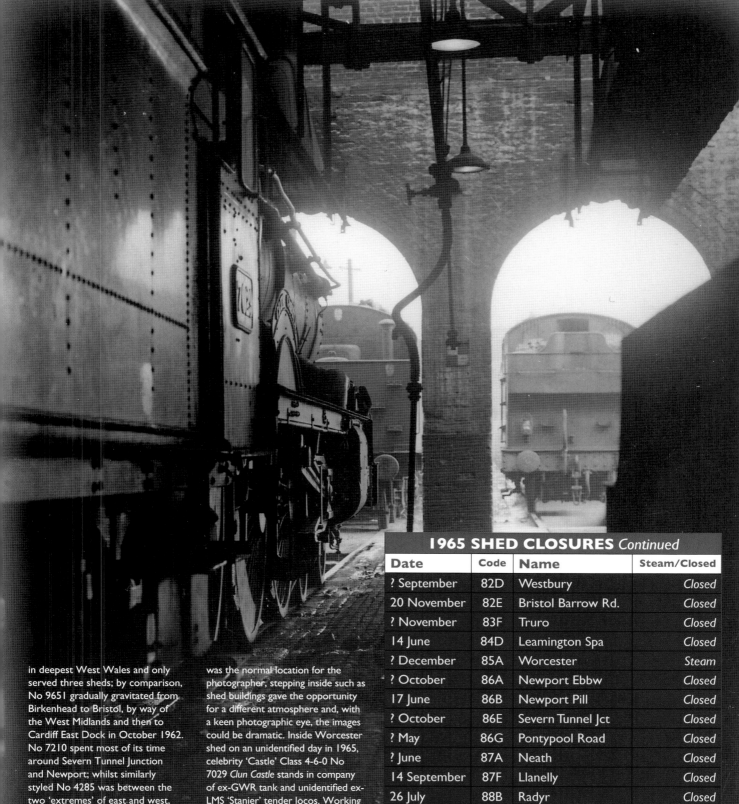

in deepest West Wales and only served three sheds; by comparison, No 9651 gradually gravitated from Birkenhead to Bristol, by way of the West Midlands and then to Cardiff East Dock in October 1962. No 7210 spent most of its time around Severn Tunnel Junction and Newport; whilst similarly styled No 4285 was between the two 'extremes' of east and west, working in and around the Valleys. *MJS collection*

Right: **Worcester:** The steam locomotive was not only attractive and emotionally charged when in full steam, but it had an inherent aesthetic appeal even when quietly at rest. Whilst the open air

was the normal location for the photographer, stepping inside such as shed buildings gave the opportunity for a different atmosphere and, with a keen photographic eye, the images could be dramatic. Inside Worcester shed on an unidentified day in 1965, celebrity 'Castle' Class 4-6-0 No 7029 *Clun Castle* stands in company of ex-GWR tank and unidentified ex-LMS 'Stanier' tender locos. Working from Gloucester (Horton Road) shed at this time, No 7029 was withdrawn on 15 January 1966. In happier times, when working the top link routes and diagrams, it was an incumbent of Newton Abbot, Laira (Plymouth) and Old Oak Common sheds amongst others. Happily, preservation beckoned. *MJS collection*

1965 SHED CLOSURES *Continued*			
Date	**Code**	**Name**	**Steam/Closed**
? September	82D	Westbury	*Closed*
20 November	82E	Bristol Barrow Rd.	*Closed*
? November	83F	Truro	*Closed*
14 June	84D	Leamington Spa	*Closed*
? December	85A	Worcester	*Steam*
? October	86A	Newport Ebbw	*Closed*
17 June	86B	Newport Pill	*Closed*
? October	86E	Severn Tunnel Jct	*Closed*
? May	86G	Pontypool Road	*Closed*
? June	87A	Neath	*Closed*
14 September	87F	Llanelly	*Closed*
26 July	88B	Radyr	*Closed*
? March	88D	Rhymney	*Closed*
1 March	88F	Treherbert	*Closed*
1 March	88J	Aberdare	*Closed*
2 August	88L	Cardiff East Dock	*Closed*
18 January	89D	Oswestry	*Closed*

1968
THE END
OF STEAM
2008

Right **Highbridge:** There were many sad casualties on our railway system in 1966, one of the top three being the since much lamented Somerset & Dorset Joint Railway (S&D). If the volume of traffic on the route had been this strong in day-to-day operations, it is conceivable that the line could have survived and any intimation of closure would have been vigorously combated.

At its height, Highbridge, with its close proximity and a connecting link to the GWR Bristol-Exeter main line, in addition to the S&D line running through and onwards to Burnham on Sea, was graced with five platforms. Many trains terminated here, however and used the bay platforms to the left of this view. Some idea of the extent of the station site can be judged from this view from 5 March 1966, as LCGB's Somerset & Dorset Railtour rests in the platform. Like some latter-day Pied Piper, Inspector Kitcher strides along the platform, with his posse following on behind!

Having set out from Waterloo behind 'Merchant Navy' Class 4-6-2 No 35028 *Clan Line* on time at 8.55 a.m., the train was double headed from Templecombe to Highbridge behind Class '2' 2-6-2T Nos 41307 and 41249, arriving here ten minutes early, at 12.35 p.m. The return trip began eight minutes down, however – no doubt in part due to restoring the tour members to their seats! – and from there things went downhill as regards timetabling. Some of this was operational constraints, but as two extra photo stops were added to the trip – at Chilcompton and Shepton Mallet – the travellers were probably not unduly concerned. Arrival back at Waterloo, again behind *Clan Line*, from Bournemouth, was at 10.10 p.m., 1½ hours late! The following day was the last day of trains on the S&D, the closure date being Monday, 7 March. Still being a relatively new

loco, having only been released from Works on 3 December 1949, No 41249 had been a Kentish Town resident for the first four years, before moving to Templecombe in 1953, for service over the S&D. Subsequent moves saw it in Bristol, Barnstaple, Plymouth and finally back to Templecombe. Allocated to the latter at the time of this tour, it was withdrawn just 22 days later. In contrast, junior by 2½ years No 41307, new on 30 June 1952, was a Southern engine for the whole of its life bar the last nine months. Initially at Three Bridges and then Exmouth Junction, the move to Templecombe came on 13 June 1965. Like its sister here, it was withdrawn 22 days after this tour.

Inset below **Bath (Green Park):** As we have already seen, the S&DR closed w.e.f. 7 March 1966 and as a result, the two remaining ex-S&D sheds ceased operations. This view of Bath (Green Park) on 5 March shows that the facility was open for business right to the end, with some of its allocation handling normal services as well as servicing visiting specials. 'Standard' Class 4 2-6-4T No 80043 has steam to spare, left, which cannot be said for most of

the other engines lined up around the shed building. 'Standard' 'Class 4s' and a '5' and a Stanier 8F are among those now cast aside by the railway and most will be going to the knacker's yard. Note the ancient grounded coach bodies, serving as day-to-day staff accommodation and the human bodies – even down to a babe in arms – casually wandering over the tracks!

1966

We won the World Cup, but...

...We lost 1966

The much loved Somerset & Dorset

Below **Bath:**
When the Permanent Way becomes not so permanent. There are many things that have disappeared in this seemingly commonplace view, apart from the rails that no longer head for the trainshed in the middle distance. We are looking towards Bath (Green Park) station from the local signalbox on 5 March 1966, again just two days from the end of passenger services. Bodies wander casually around the tracks; a line of locomotives stands outside the shed building; goods wagons (admittedly empty in this view!) fill the sidings; the ancient corrugated hut and gas lamp belong to a past era; carriage stock stands around

Your authors were faced with an impossible choice when considering which aspects of the railway to select for inclusion in this volume. Quite clearly in trying to convey to readers young and old alike it was important to try and distil out the very essence of the railways during the mid-sixties - not unlike the blending of a fine whisky or the combining of ingredients in a recipe to create the taste and flavour in one's mind. The loss of the Somerset & Dorset line from Bath Green Park through to Bournemouth Central on 7 March 1966 was an event that simply had to be recorded within these pages.

Readers may recall the evocative black and white BBC documentary filmed in 1962 and narrated by John Betjeman entitled *The Branch Line Railway*. Drawing attention to the impending closure of this and so many other

the station throat; and the point rodding and semaphore signals all seem so permanent.

Built in 1870 by the Midland Railway, as a terminus of the line from Mangotsfield and originally named Queen Square, the deliberately

elegant style was to blend in with the Georgian buildings of the city that overlooked it. The S&D joined the layout in 1874, giving the MR a route from the Midlands to the south coast; and its final name was bestowed by BR in 1954. Closure was ordained by the infamous Dr

Beeching. The vaulted glass roof in a single-span wrought iron arch was a telltale feature and still remains today, as cover for the car park of Sainsbury's supermarket, as does the bridge over the River Avon, now acting as entrance to that car park.

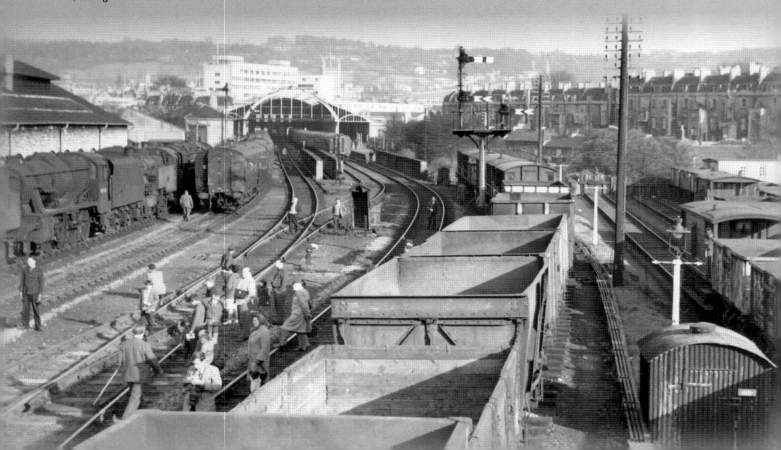

4-6-2 No 34057 *Biggin Hill*, a mere nine minutes behind time. Tour participants were allowed just short of an hour to sample the delights of the station and shed – or, if they desired, the city – during which time the two Pacifics (both allocated to Salisbury at this date and both destined to survive to very close to the end of steam on BR(SR) the following year) were turned and serviced. In this view, No 34006 is turned and ready to rejoin its sister and looks a model of respectability and competence. To the right Class '4' 2-6-4T No 80043 stands outside the shed between duties, blowing off excess boiler pressure, watched by some of the visitors. A mere teenager when seen here, it was new on 9 August 1952 to Bletchley shed for the first seven years of its life. Having transferred allegiance to the SR in December 1959, it served various sheds before washing up at Templecombe in October 1964. Its end, with so many of the S&D servants was ordained on 27 March 1966, three weeks from this view.

Top: There is no doubting where we are! Originally opened 3 February 1862 as "Evercreech" on the original S&D line from Burnham-on-Sea to Broadstone, it became from 20 July 1874 the junction for the northwards extension towards Bath that eventually bankrupted the company. A station that was much nearer to the village of Evercreech opened on the Bath extension more than a mile to the north of Evercreech Junction, was initially called Evercreech Village, and later Evercreech New. The junction itself was to the north of the station, where there were also marshalling yards. Branch trains to and from Burnham and Highbridge started and finished at Evercreech in latter years. To the south of the station a level crossing carried the main A371 road across the line. Goods traffic was withdrawn from the station on 29 November 1965, leaving the station to close completely in 1966 with the closure of the whole line as part of the Beeching axe. The nearby station inn was renamed as *The Silent Whistle* on the closure of the line. Beyond the station sign, in this view, the Junction Café has a veritable collection of period vehicles standing outside. Notice the hedge alongside the station fence and the small, but now empty, rockery.

Below Briefly back at Bath (Green Park), we are now on shed. The LCGB Somerset & Dorset Rail Tour of 5 March, already seen on *Page 36*, arrived at Bath behind 'West Country' Class 4-6-2 No 34006 *Bude* and 'Battle of Britain' Class

branch lines John was filmed travelling from Evercreech Junction through to Highbridge & Burnham-on-Sea the 24 mile branch line that eventually closed on 19 February 1966 - a few months earlier than the main line. In spite of this impassioned plea and that of thousands of others the rails were ripped up and another valuable asset and transport link were lost. No more would the sound of steam working hard on the climb out of Bath and up through the Mendips be heard and seen. This was a line that had virtually everything an enthusiast could wish for! Operationally interesting with for example, the use of banking engines helping longer trains up the stiffer gradients and the unusual reversal of passenger trains at Templecombe, so as to avoid a walk of over half a mile between the two stations at this important intersection.

The main line from Bath to Bournemouth (West) was a little over 71 miles and passed through some of Britain's finest countryside, crossing the lush green rolling hills and farmland on its way to the seaside. The line was busiest not surprisingly in the summer months with trains travelling from as far afield as Manchester, Leeds, Bradford, Preston, St. Helens, Liverpool, Derby, Birmingham, Gloucester and Cheltenham.

Main picture **A study in concentration**, on the footplate of 'Battle of Britain' Class 4-6-2 No 34057 *Biggin Hill* during the LCGB tour already highlighted. One does not have to be a genius to immediately recognise the difference in status between the two men! To the right, Driver A. Williams (of Bath [Green Park]) has his eye well and truly on the road, whilst behind him, the road and driver are both of serious concern to Inspector Crowley of Nine Elms. Appearances can be deceiving, however and the crews and Inspectors normally had a close and genial working relationship, as both wanted the best from locomotive and for the public and the nominally more senior man had more than likely worked his way through the ranks.

Left: Another view from a train on the S&D — and one partly powered by Class '4' 2-6-4T No 80043 seen on *page 34* — but a month prior to the LCGB outing. On 26 February 1966, the photographer rode from Bournemouth to Shepton Mallet and on the way captured this view of the station sign at Glastonbury and Street. As can be seen, he was not graced with such kind weather as the later LCGB tour! *Gerald Adams/ MJS collection*

The Somerset & Dorset - Down Main Line

Miles	Chains	Station/location
0	0	Bath Green Park Station
0	41	Bath junction
4	29	Midford
6	61	Wellow
8	46	Shoscombe & SH Halt
10	52	Radstock
12	42	Midsomer Norton
14	39	Chilcompton
17	5	Binegar
18	51	Masbury Halt
21	68	Shepton Mallet
24	72	Evercreech New
26	34	Evercreech Jct Station
29	16	Cole
33	36	Wincanton
36	79	Templecombe Lower
37	7	Templecombe Upper
36	54	Templecombe No 2 Junction
		Templecombe Lower
36	68	Henstridge
40	27	Staibridge
44	25	Sturminster Newton
47	28	Shillingstone
49	54	Stourpaine Loop
50	13	Stourpaine & D Halt
52	65	Blandford
54	41	Charlton Marshall Halt
56	9	Spetisbury
58	74	Bailey Gate
60	56	Corfe Mullen Signal Box
62	0	Corfe Mullen Halt
63	56	Broadstone
65	1	Creekmoor Halt
67	11	Poole
68	75	Parkstone
70	20	Branksome
71	38	Bournemouth West

A daily service from Manchester to Bournemouth introduced way back in October 1910 became the routes most famous train *The Pines Express,* so named because of the many pine trees to be found in the resort area of Bournemouth and Poole. *The Pines* first ran under that name on 26 September 1927 and grew in popularity over the years that followed with additional portions from Sheffield and Liverpool being added to the Manchester train in later years. In the busiest periods separate trains from the destinations would be run, each claiming to be *The Pines Express!* The last *Pines* to run over the S&D route was on 8 September 1962 hauled by Class '9F' 2-10-0 No 92220 *Evening Star,* the last steam locomotive built for British Railways at their Swindon workshops and new to traffic in March 1960 a mere two years before. Happily unlike the S&D or the *Pines Express, Evening Star* survives as part of The National Collection.

When originally opened the Main Line was actually from Burnham-on-Sea to Bournemouth and Poole the intention having been to provide an 'International route' linking Wales with France and the rest of the European rail network! This was to be achieved with ferries from South Wales crossing the Bristol Channel landing at the pier at Burnham-on-Sea from where passengers and freight would be carried to Poole Harbour and onwards by ferries across the channel. Sadly these grand plans were never fully realised and the more lucrative route from Evercreech to Bath became the Main line leaving the rails to Burnham-on-Sea as one of three S&D branches.

Main picture: Another view of the 5 March railtour out on the line, this time between Evercreech New and Shepton Mallet stations. Taken at 200th of a second, with an aperture setting of f8, the photographer has done well to successfully capture the image, keeping the verticals in appropriate alignment, the locomotives at an optimum position as they approach a reverse curve and to highlight the excitement of the photographers hanging out of every available window to capture the scene for themselves! 'West Country' Class 4-6-2 No 34006 *Bude* and 'Battle of Britain' Class 4-6-2 No 34057 *Biggin Hill* are in fine style here, with clean white smoke betraying that both firemen are on top of their jobs and that the locos themselves are in good condition. Surprisingly, bearing in mind the occasion and compared to what a similar 'last day' run would engender today, there are no swarms of camera-toting bodies patrolling the fields to record their own images of the trip.

Right **Chilcompton:** A second view of the photo stop at Chilcompton shows the view looking back along the train and track and identifying something of the incline here. 34057 seems to be wasting some of its potential power at this juncture, with an unusual show of dark smoke as it stands waiting for the off.
No 34006 is the elder of the two, emerging from Brighton Works in July 1945 and had only three homes before withdrawal, from Salisbury, in March 1967. In surviving to that date, the locomotive outlasted the other railway connection with Bude, as the branch line to the town lost its rail service on 1 October 1966 – five months after this view and 68 years after the link was first forged in 1898. Note the virtually unmarked white buffers, especially painted for the day.

Branch: (Down) Burnham-on-Sea - Evercreech Jct.		
Miles	Chains	Station/Location
0	0	Burnham-on-Sea
1	50	Highbridge
3	21	Bason Bridge
6	60	Edington Junction
8	74	Shapwick
10	67	Ashcott
13	43	Glastonbury & Street
18	66	West Pennard
22	17	Pylle
23	75	Evercreech North Jct.
24	19	Evercreech Station

The others being those to Wells (Closed to all traffic 29 October 1951) and Bridgwater (Closed to Passengers 1 December 1952 and Goods from 1 October 1954)

Branches (Down) Wells - Glastonbury & Street - Bridgwater		
Miles	Chains	Station/location
0	0	Wells
2	30	Polsham Halt
5	33	Glastonbury & Street
17	39	Edington junction
20	42	Cossington
21	53	Bawdrip Halt
24	54	Bridgwater

The line had been part of the Southern Region from Nationalisation in 1948 through to 1958 but was then transferred to the Western Region. This meant motive power

on the route was a rich and varied mixture. Just a few of the more common examples to be found working the line in the latter years were the following:

Ex S&DJR Class 7F 2-8-0s
Ex S&DJR Class 4F 0-6-0 tender locos
Ex-LMS 0-6-0 Jinties
Ex-SR West Country Class
Ex-SR Battle of Britain Class
Ex-GWR 2251 Class 0-6-0s
Ex-GWR 5700 Class 0-6-0 Pannier Tanks
BR Standard Class 3 2-6-2s
BR Standard Class 4 4-6-0s,
BR Standard Class 5 4-6-0s
BR Standard Class 4 2-6-4T
BR Standard Class 9F 2-10-0s

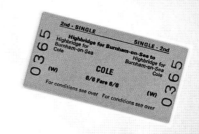

Once the Western Region powers that be moved *The Pines Express* to run over the Ex Great Western/Southern route via Oxford, Reading, Basingstoke and Southampton (also to Poole in the final two years), the writing was very much on the wall for the S&D. Sadly the last normal passenger trains ran on 7 March 1966. Track lifting along most of the route took place between March and May of 1967 ending any hope of a reinstatement of services - although even to the present day there are those who believe one day...! The last *Pines Express* on the new route ran on 4 March 1967 just as track lifting started on the S&D.

It is still possible to enjoy elements of the S&D and here are just a few examples:

• There is a thriving Museum at Washford Station on The West Somerset Railway run by The Somerset & Dorset Railway Trust.

• Midsommer Norton Station is also undergoing restoration and has a growing visitor centre.

• Shillingstone Station has been saved and is now being enthusiastically restored to a high standard by the North Dorset Railway Trust.

Below inset: As already seen at Highbridge on *Page 35*, part of the tour was handled by Class '2' 2-6-2T Nos 41307 and 41249 double-headed. They are seen here at around 12 noon, during an impromptu ten-minute photo stop. Although from the same Class, there are detail differences between the two locos, not least the fact that No 41307 is in fully lined livery, whereas No 41249 is devoid any such adornment; the chimneys are different, with No 41307 having a slightly taller version; No 41249's top-feed cover is missing its 'cap'; piping along the tank top is not identical; and the guttering on the cab roof is of different design modes. The inspector casually walks alongside, no doubt casting an experienced eye on things, but the crew of 41307 do not seem unduly perturbed. Both locos have plenty of steam for the rest of their share of the run, to Highbridge and then back to Evercreech Junction.

Above: Fireman's eye view! We are again on board the 5 March LCGB tour, out in the S&D countryside, thought to be between Radstock and Bath. Enjoying his very privileged position, riding on the footplate of 'Battle of Britain' Class 4-6-2 No 34057 *Biggin Hill*, our intrepid photographer takes advantage of no approaching crossing trains or bridges or other structures that could have impeded him! Note the unusual close-up view of Mr Bullied's air-smoothed boiler casing.

Below right **Chilcompton:** Earlier in the day, there was an unscheduled stop at Glastonbury and Chilcompton on the outward run and the latter is seen here in the early afternoon. This had the effect of lengthening the journey time from Binegar (to the south) and Radstock (to the north) from nine minutes to twenty-two! We have already seen No 34006 at Bath, we now have a closer view of 'Battle of Britain' Class 4-6-2 No 34057 *Biggin Hill*. One of the remaining stock of Bullied's 'Pacifics' still unrebuilt, No 34057 was new in May 1947, ninth on the Class named after celebrated people and places connected with the Battle of Britain. RAF Biggin Hill, on the southern outskirts of London, served as one of the principal fighter bases protecting London and South East England from attack by enemy bombers. Over the course of WWII, fighters based at the airfield claimed 1,400 enemy aircraft, at the cost of the lives of 453 Biggin

Hill based aircrew. It was one of the commanding bases for the Battle of Britain, with both Spitfires and Hurricanes from a variety of squadrons being based there and, because of its importance to the capital's defence, the airport itself became a target. Between August 1940 and January 1941, it was attacked twelve times, the worst of which wrecked workshops, stores, barracks, WAAF quarters and a hangar, killing 39 people on the ground. The loco served a number of prestigious BR(SR) sheds to the end, but perhaps the strangest event was the transfer to Stratford, in

east London, on BR(ER) for twelve months from May 1951 to May 1952! Surviving until the very last few months of steam on the SR, it was withdrawn, from Salisbury, on 15 May 1967, exactly 20 years old.

Interestingly David Porter the eventual saviour of 'Black 5' 4-6-0 No 45110 *(see pages 132-139)* had wanted to purchase No 34057 for preservation but which had unfortunately been sold for scrap, due to an apparent administrative mix up of loco numbers, before he could secure her.

wall for the Great Central from the late 1950s, with the opening of the first section of the M1 motorway – between junction 5 (Watford) and junction 18 (Crick/Rugby) – on 2 November 1959. Running north from the latter junction from 1965, it paralleled the GCR for much of the way through south Leicestershire and can been seen here in the background. Would that the traffic could be this sparse today! On 9 May 1966, 'Black 5' Class 4-6-0 No 44936 runs into Ashby Magna station with the 4.38 p.m. Marylebone-Nottingham (Victoria) semi-fast. Note the typical GCR station architecture still in place; and the recently lifted goods loop, in the foreground, that has been very tidily left by the engineers. The very rural nature of the line is well exemplified in this view. *Mike Mitchell*

Above **Barnston Summit:** In the latter years of the Great Central, the erstwhile Marylebone-Manchester expresses were no more and those trains that still ran into and out of the London terminus only travelled as far as Nottingham. By and large they were three-coach semi-fasts, with a limited number of stops and, in the main, hauled by Stanier's "Black 5's'. Gone were the recent heady days of 'Royal Scots' and 'Britannias' that had taken the place of B1s, V2s and even A3s and, inevitably, many photographers, too, moved on to more enticing vistas. On 31 May

1966, the 6.15 p.m. Nottingham (Victoria)-Rugby (Central) stopper was one such example, seen behind 'Black 5' Class 4-6-0 No 44876 as it climbs to Barnston Summit, with the fireman taking a breather from his exertions in providing his driver with sufficient steam. This was an unusual loco to be working the GCR, as it was allocated to Oxley (Wolverhampton) at this time and most motive power on the route operated from local sheds. Perhaps Nottingham had 'seconded' the engine during a visit to the city and Annesley shed being short of power? A resident of Carlisle

(Upperby) shed at the formation of British Railways, it would move south to Aston (Birmingham) on 6 October 1951 and stayed there until October 1965 when it travelled the relatively short distance to Wolverhampton and Oxley shed. Thereafter, Chester was favoured from March 1967, then Stoke one month later and Birkenhead four months after that. It did not quite make it to the last year of steam on BR, being taken from active stock on 2 December 1967. *Mike Mitchell*

Below: Thanks to Mr Marples and his cronies, the writing was on the

Main picture **Newton:** Colour does add to the appreciation of the more mundane view, but it also tends to highlight any deterioration in either motive power or carriage stock. The former is the case here, as 'Black 5' Class 4-6-0 No 45426 heads away from the camera near Newton, north of Rugby (Central). The date is 5 March 1966 and the train is another local, this time

...We lost

1966

The old Great Central Main Line

the 12.30 p.m. Rugby (Central)-Leicester (Central). The external condition of the 'Black 5' exemplifies the general standard maintained throughout the UK at this time, when, in so many cases, it was as much as a shedmaster could do to keep sufficient stock in working order to fulfil the duty rosters!

No 45426 was another well travelled loco, working from Patricroft at the birth of BR and serving a whole host of WCML sheds from Manchester to London, ending up at Edge Hill (Liverpool) on 20 August 1966, from where it went the way of all flesh on 23 March 1968. Its stay on the GCR was short, from 19 February 1966 to that move to Edge Hill and, consequently, this was another of the rarer visitors to the route.
Mike Mensing

The Great Central Railway was unique in three ways:

• it was the last main line to be built, many years after its predecessors/competitors.

• It was the only railway that was constructed with plans to run right through to Europe via a Channel Tunnel and, thus, built to the Continental Berne Gauge.

• It was the only main line to have its own 'tame' photographer, in the guise of S W A Newton, who recorded on camera the construction of and the people concerned before, during and after opening.

It was also built with easy gradients, with no major inclines or gradients, compared to some of its neighbours. South of Nottingham, summits were between Ashby Magna and Lutterworth stations and at Charwelton and the steepest gradients for any length of time was normally no more than 1-in-176; and there was no curve of less than a mile radius; but its great weakness was that, for the most part, it passed through very rural countryside, with the major conurbations already well served by existing lines, leaving little room for the new interloper.

CHRIS WARD
*Fireman at Annesley shed
on the ex-Great Central*
Remembers...

*I first started being interested in trains
around 1952. (I know that because
one of the first namers I saw was B1
4-6-0 No 61029 Chamois (which was
transferred from Sheffield Darnall
(41A) to St.Margarets (64A) in 1953).
I was seven years old and used to walk
from my home to Hucknall National
Junior School. As I crossed the bridge over the GC I used to wait at around 08.30
for the 'Master Cutler' on its southbound journey to London Marylebone. It was
always headed by one of Leicester's (38C) A3, nos. 60049 Galtee More, 60052
Prince Palatine, 60054 Prince of Wales, 60102 Sir Frederick Banbury, 60104
Solario and 60107 Royal Lancer. Then it was run like mad to get to school before
assembly at 08.55! Thereafter, all available spare time was spent on the fence
outside Hucknall Central Station!*

*The only job I ever wanted to do was to be an engine driver, so after a brief
interview with Mr. Ede, the Shedmaster, and a subsequent medical at Derby, I
started my working life at Annesley at 08.00 on January 11th 1960. On arrival
at the Depot I was kitted out with overalls and grease top cap and introduced to
Fred Lees, the Chargehand cleaner. To say Fred was surprised to see me was an
understatement! I was the first cleaner since Annesley was taken under the Midland
Region's wing in 1958! Fred was also in charge of the labouring force and he sent
me over to the canteen, while he decided what to do with me!*

*After about an hour I was sent to the stores to get a bucket of paraffin and some
washed rags, to clean all the cab numbers of the Annesley engines that were on
shed. I was told I could do this all week and, so long as I kept out of the way, I
could go more or less anywhere and do almost anything I liked! All this for the
princely sum of £3 17s 6d per week!*

*After my first (and only) week cleaning, as the eldest (and only) cleaner, Fred said
I would now be labouring, and I was given charge of sweeping roads 1, 2 and 3 as
far as the water columns at the end of the shed front. I was convinced that I was
on my way to my first million! The labourers' rate of pay was £8 8s 0d per week
- this was as much as my dad earned at Hucknall No 2 colliery, and all my mates
were earning about £3 a week! I knew that, as the eldest hand, as soon as I was
sixteen I would also get firing opportunities, so, Saturday, December 10th 1960
and the great day had arrived! My sixteenth birthday and my first firing turns.*

*During the first month or so, my forays on the main line were limited to
(1) travelling to Bulwell Common on the railway bus, to relieve crews whose eight
hours were up.
(2) Relieving 'runners' at Annesley South Junction and taking them onward to local
collieries. (Incidentally, the term 'runners' was used together with 'windcutters' to*

The Marylebone terminus – often referred to as 'the
gentleman's station, because of its smallness in size
compared to the other London termini – opened for business
on 9 March 1899 but, beyond these bald facts there is a
fascinating and heroic history. Many other volumes have been
dedicated to this story, but an overview is appropriate and
desirable here.

L T C Rolt eloquently commented in the Introduction to his
book, *The Making of a Railway* (Sutton Publishing), "There was
never any 'rush hour' worthy of the name at Marylebone and
no one ever seemed to be in a hurry. Standing in its quiet,
spacious concourse, cut off from the fretful sound of the
traffic in the Marylebone Road by the huge bulk of the Great

Above **East Leake:** 'Black 5' Class
4-6-0 No 45426, seen on the last
page, is again in view, this time
three months later and looking little
improved from the previous shot. In
bright sunshine of June 1966, there
are just two whole months left for
the GCR and yet the 'Black 5' has
a much greater consist attached to
it. In a deep cutting at East Leake,
once the next station stop north of
Loughborough (Central), the train
has seven coaches and is, therefore,
unlikely to be an ordinary service,
but rather is more probably a
special working. The heads from
the front coach would seem to
reinforce this assumption. Being
only on the GCR for six months,
the loco was presumably worked
hard in view of the frequency
in photographs of the era. *MJS
collection*

Right **Newton:** Here it is again!
Once again showing the disreputable
condition seen on *page 45*, the
12.30 Rugby (Central)-Leicester
(Central) stopping service is again
seen, this time seen approaching
the camera near Newton, north
of Rugby. The fireman has his
arm resting on the cab sidesheet
between bouts with the shovel.
Even with a stop at Lutterworth,
the journey would only have taken
around 30 minutes between the
two towns, a time that would have
been difficult to beat by road. *Mike
Mensing*

**LADIES
ROOM**

Central Hotel across the forecourt, you half expected to hear the sound of cathedral bells. Even the arrival or departure of its not-too-frequent trains scarcely disturbed this atmosphere of cloistered calm. …..The peace of Marylebone boded ill for Great Central shareholders, but it certainly made things very pleasant for the railways' patrons, making them feel as though they were members of some exclusive club." And it was this peace – and latterday railway politics – that was to be the undoing of the railway.

O ne of your authors knew the erstwhile GCR in its last decade – from when he would rush at lunchtime from school to Loughborough Central station, to see the 'A3s' on the up *The South Yorkshireman* express, as it made the brief stop at the station in 1955 - to closure in 1966. Travelling by train from Syston to Loughborough, in his first two years of 'big school', he would stand on the southern end of Loughborough Midland station and watch the trains go over the bridge that crossed the Midland Main Line. He would also join his grandfather at his

describe the Annesley to Woodford out and home service, ('windcutters dating from pre-war days!). My frst proper main line trip came in February 1961, when I was booked with driver George Thompson, on the 13.55 'Spare'. I was just brewing our frst can of tea of the day, when Running Foreman Lol Crampton, said, "63886 (an ex-L.N.E.R. O1 2-8-0) is on the shed front, she's all ready - Special to Wichnor." So off we went and backed on to our train of coke for Wichnor Junction, south of Burton (on the despised Midland Railway)! I remember feeling ten feet tall, waving to the trainspotters on Burton Station! Little did we know that by the end of 1962, all our "O1's" would be withdrawn en masse and replaced by ex-LMS "8F" 2-8-0's!

One of the most important lessons I learned in my early cleaning days was that you never, ever, spat on the footplate! The motto "cleanliness is next to godliness" stayed with me all through my firing days, and I can proudly say that my footplates were always spotless. As a passed cleaner, I fired on the Queens Walk Goods Pilot turn and I occasionally had an ex -Great Northern engine - (L.N.E.R. J6 0-6-0 No 64219 was one). You had to take two steps with each shovelful of coal to put it in the firebox! God knows how Leicester men used to get from Belgrave Road to Skegness on these old Crates!

I could go on at length, but space here has precluded many more, mostly happy, memories.

Right **Midland Red:** Back in the age of steam and when the Great Central route was still open the many connecting bus services in the Leicester and Loughborough area were in the hands of the *Birmingham and Midland Motor Omnibus Company* or *Midland Red*. A period piece still in use at Bridgnorth station on the Severn Valley Railway is this timetable holder. *PT*

Below **Culworth:** Still out in the countryside on the Great Central, we have now moved to Banbury Lane, south of Culworth, to see 'Black 5' Class 4-6-0 No 44936 on the 2.38 p.m. Marylebone-Nottingham (Victoria) semi-fast of 26 March 1966. Close to Culworth Junction, the train would soon meet the once-active branch to

Banbury that enabled cross-country services to be so successful over the GCR lines. Here graced with four coaches, the train would take roughly two hours to Rugby and a further 30 minutes to Leicester, before finally arriving at Nottingham at approximately 5.40 p.m. With a little effort these timings could have been improved, but such was the legacy of passing through sparse countryside from coming to the railway map so late in the day, in 1899, that the GCR was never going to be a massive fund raiser for its bosses.

No 44936 was yet another widely travelled loco that spent precious little time on this route. Just nine months, at Colwick between 19

February and 12 November 1966, the last two months of which saw very little action after the closure of the through route and of steam on the remaining services in September. Carlisle, Preston, Llandudno Junction, Northampton, Banbury and back to Carlisle highlights its wanderlust! Withdrawal was on 9 September 1967. *Mike Mitchell*

Opposite page **Leicester (Central):** Between Nottingham (Victoria) and Marylebone, Leicester was probably the most important stop. Built as an 'island' station on an embankment above the surrounding streets that had necessitated the demolition of many 'slum' dwellings for its location, it boasted, at its height, bays north and south for

local services, carriage sidings on either side of the facility and a turntable at the south eastern end of the station for use by the many locomotives changing here. The resulting site was extensive, with the platforms housing full facilities, including a restaurant through to latter years. Part of the massive canopies to protect passengers from the elements can be seen here on 26 August, as 'Black 5' Class 4-6-0 No 45267 arrives with the 4.38 p.m. Marylebone-Nottingham (Victoria) semi-fast, just a week from the end of steam here. Note the very few passengers that have detrained; and the removal, right, of one of the erstwhile carriage sidings. *Mike Mitchell*

allotment by the fence adjacent to Belgrave & Birstall station – collecting numbers as the trains went by – and, from 1961-63 he would escape from his work in the centre of Leicester, to partake of lunch at Central station. At all of these venues and times, there was always the relaxed air, with long periods between trains; and the air of a grand past pervaded those lunches at Leicester Central, as the buffet was still open (rather like a scene from *Brief Encounter*) and crockery and cutlery was still proudly emblazoned with the GCR monika!

Despite coming so late to the fading 'Railway Mania', there was no lack of vision. Starting out as the provincial and somewhat parochial 'Manchester, Sheffield & Lincolnshire Railway', it had grandiose designs to strike south, first to capture the Capital and then to strike onwards towards and through a (then non-existent) Channel Tunnel. The progenitor, Sir Edward Watkin, was a man in the mould of the Midland's infamous 'Railway King', George Hudson. There was logic to his plans, as he had connections with London's Metropolitan Railway, the East London Railway and the South Eastern Railway, the last two of which would take him under the Thames and down to Folkestone. His sights were most obviously on Europe, with London being a stopping point en-route. With what we have seen since its closure in 1966, it is a shame that his plan was not more successful or appreciated.

The line was never a financial success and it was swallowed within the formation of the LNER in the Grouping of 1923. This gave the new organisation a toe-hold into London through a second route and enabled it to reach areas otherwise outside its sphere, not least by the spur to Banbury and the connection to the GWR, enabling lucrative cross-country trains – passenger and freight – to flourish. However, the sparseness of the countryside and the growing development and popularity of the internal combustion engine drew the noose ever tighter. The LNER had tried to encourage patronage – and compete with its close neighbour and rival, the LMS – by operating two prestigious expresses, *The South Yorkshireman* and *The Master Cutler*, from Sheffield to Marylebone, with all the trimmings for travellers, and by transferring Gresley's 'A3s' to the services. They were successful, but Nationalisation in 1948 put paid to any future for them. Now with two main lines into London from the East Midlands, roughly parallel, British Railways sought to reduce costs. One had to go and with the transfer of the GCR route to the MR in 1958, the writing was well and truly on the wall. The expresses – much favoured by Leicester businessmen – were withdrawn in 1961; local passenger services were removed in 1963; freight largely disappeared from 1965; and the end came in September 1966.

There have been constant calls – and floated ideas – for reopening the line since, strategic as it is up the spine of the country, but too many obstacles have been placed in the way, not least by the removal of bridges, viaducts, etc., and building over part of the old trackbed. But even into 2008, there have been thoughts mooted of installing light rail along parts of the route, especially from the south into Leicestershire's county and city, but they are likely to remain pie-in-the-sky.

Left **Rushcliffe Halt:** With the lack of massive human traffic and the gradual run-down of freight services, the GCR never had a hurried feel. Gaps between trains led to a somnolent air and relaxing experiences. Momentarily shattering the peace on 18 June, 'Black 5' Class 4-6-0 No 44825 steams into Rushcliffe Halt with the 2.38 p.m. Marylebone-Nottingham service. A well travelled loco, the 'Black 5' was serving out an eleven month stay at Colwick shed and wears a stencilled 'COLK' to confirm on the smokebox front in place of a shedplate. With the end of steam on the GCR, the loco moved north to Carlisle (Kingmoor) in November, to end its days there on 7 October 1967. *Mike Mitchell*

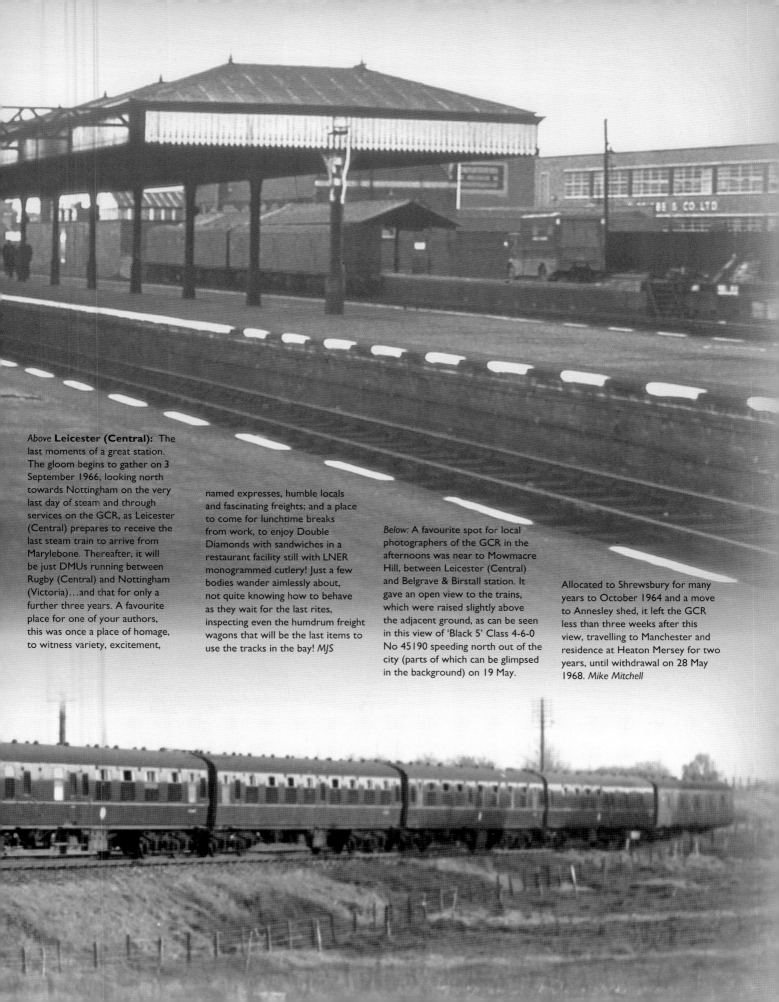

Above **Leicester (Central):** The last moments of a great station. The gloom begins to gather on 3 September 1966, looking north towards Nottingham on the very last day of steam and through services on the GCR, as Leicester (Central) prepares to receive the last steam train to arrive from Marylebone. Thereafter, it will be just DMUs running between Rugby (Central) and Nottingham (Victoria)…and that for only a further three years. A favourite place for one of your authors, this was once a place of homage, to witness variety, excitement, named expresses, humble locals and fascinating freights; and a place to come for lunchtime breaks from work, to enjoy Double Diamonds with sandwiches in a restaurant facility still with LNER monogrammed cutlery! Just a few bodies wander aimlessly about, not quite knowing how to behave as they wait for the last rites, inspecting even the humdrum freight wagons that will be the last items to use the tracks in the bay! *MJS*

Below: A favourite spot for local photographers of the GCR in the afternoons was near to Mowmacre Hill, between Leicester (Central) and Belgrave & Birstall station. It gave an open view to the trains, which were raised slightly above the adjacent ground, as can be seen in this view of 'Black 5' Class 4-6-0 No 45190 speeding north out of the city (parts of which can be glimpsed in the background) on 19 May.

Allocated to Shrewsbury for many years to October 1964 and a move to Annesley shed, it left the GCR less than three weeks after this view, travelling to Manchester and residence at Heaton Mersey for two years, until withdrawal on 28 May 1968. *Mike Mitchell*

Left **Belgrave & Birstall:** Abandoned! The footpath, right, that ran alongside the railway was a favourite spotter's venue, close by Belgrave & Birstall station. The proximity of the signalbox, just out of sight to the left, with its concert of bells, was advantageous for being aware of approaching trains and your photographer spent many hours here, next to his grandfather's allotment. Two weeks to the day after closure of the GCR as a through route, the station still looks in fine shape on 17 September, but it has been closed as a public facility for a few years and will not see trains stop here again. Post-1969, when the Main Line Steam Trust were formulating plans to restore trains

to this point, it was hoped to re-use the station, but vandals saw off that idea, to the end that a completely new station was needed when what became Leicester North was finally reached from Loughborough by the new GCR. *MJS*

Above & below **Culworth:** Another view of the last day, with this time the train heading for Marylebone. The 5.15 p.m. Nottingham (Victoria)-Marylebone wears a wreath to

Following closure, *The Main Line Steam Trust* was formed to salvage what they could. They have progressively reopened and developed the only preserved main line route in the UK, between Loughborough (Central) and what was Belgrave & Birstall station – now called Leicester North. They go from strength to strength, with plans to again cross the MML and strike out towards Nottingham, joining up with the group forging their way south from Ruddington.

'celebrate' the occasion as it passes the site of Culworth station on 3 September. Behind 'Black 5' Class 4-6-0 No 44984 are at least eight coaches, each full of gricers capturing and savouring the moment and with many manning the windows! The last main line built in the UK, much with easy gradients and constructed to the Berne gauge, with ideas of through trains to Europe via a Channel tunnel, it had the potential – sadly never realised – of being a

world-beater. Forty years later, there have been many calls for the layout to be re-used.

No 44984 spent much of its life roaring up and down the MML north of St Pancras but had come to the GCR late in the day, on Christmas Day 1965. Operating out of Colwick, it is here having the honour of the last through train south, after which it retired to its home shed to await withdrawal, which came on 3 December 1966. *Both Mike Mensing*

All change on the Isle of Wight!

Above Passing at Brading. In June 1966, the holiday season is in full swing on the island and, on the surface, there is nothing that would herald the end just six months later. In the early afternoon sunshine, Class 'O2' 0-4-4T No14 *Fishbourne's* fireman leans out to release the token he has held from Ryde, whilst Class 'O2' 0-4-4T No17 *Seaview* waits for the 'right away' and its journey north to that terminus. Respectively ex-L&SWR 178 and 208, they came to the island in 1936 and 1930 and both were to be survivors to the end. *Geoff King*

Opposite top left **Ryde (Esplanade):** The Isle of Wight's railway adventure began in 1859, with the incorporation of the Cowes & Newport Railway on 8 August. Expansion saw the optimum spider's web of lines reached from June 1900, when the final short extension into Ventnor opened. This layout had a life of a little over half a century before economics really began to bite. The line from Merstone to Ventnor West was the first to go, on 15 September 1952, after which other parts withered and fell off the tree until the only stretch left was that between Ryde and Shanklin. By

Thankfully The Isle of Wight Steam Railway based at Havenstreet near Ryde were able to step in and save a stretch of the erstwhile Newport to Ryde line and in doing so have preserved the very essence of what was for so many people part of their growing up!

The Isle of Wight is still of course very much a holiday destination, but in the years before first 'every family had a motor car' and second the advent of cheap air fares and overseas package holidays, the island was a very different place. Right up to the late 1950s and early 1960s paddle and conventional steam vessels would ply their trade from ports along the south coast including variously - Bournemouth, Lymington, Weymouth, Poole, Southampton, Portsmouth and Southsea. Excursion sailings were popular in addition to the traditional ferry service.

Landing at Ryde, Cowes and Yarmouth these ships would disgorge thousands of visitors and locals alike on to the piers and jetties - it was imperative that they be moved as quickly as possible! Safety dictated it if nothing else, as the next wave (usually of people or freight!) would not be far behind. The railways on the island were built between 1862 and 1900 to cope with the growing trade and the need to transport both passengers and freight to all strategic points on the island. The network at its height consisted of the following routes:

the time enthusiasts really became aware of this 'progress', there was relatively little left to photograph. Steam ceased on BR services on 31 December 1966. Just three months from the end, Class 'O2' 0-4-4T No24 *Calbourne* stands at Ryde (Esplanade) station, waiting to take the short trip over the water to Pier station. Luggage waits by the engine for inclusion on the train. *Frank Cassell*

Left **Ventnor Town:** Without doubt, the most challenging structure on any of the island's railways was the tunnel giving access to Ventnor Town station. Carving through the 787ft St. Boniface Down – the highest point on the island – the last few yards of rails then ended at a facility resting high above the town they purported to serve. Post-Victorian times, the town became a regular holiday destination and, with its warm microclimate occasioned

by the surrounding cliffs, was a magnet for sufferers of tuberculosis. Several sanatoria were established in Ventnor for those suffering from the disease; and at one point Charles Dickens was a local resident (though not of a sanatorium!). In this view from the last few months of operation in 1966, the diminutive nature of the tunnel can be seen, with it, signalbox and semaphore signals all dwarfed by the Downs. *Dennis Weaver/MJS collection*

* Ryde - Smallbrook Junction - Brading - Sandown - Shanklin - Ventnor.
* Brading - Bembridge.
* Cowes - Newport - Merstone - Sandown.
* Merstone - Ventnor (West).
* Newport - Havenstreet - Wootton - Ashey - Smallbrook Junction.
* Newport - Yarmouth - Freshwater.

This meant that every town and most large villages were either on or near a railway. Much has been written about the notion that saving our railways or campaigning to have them reinstated is somehow 'living in the past' or bemoaning a romantic bygone era... If ever there was a case for consideration as to the sensibility, in hindsight, of ripping up an asset that our forbearers toiled and struggled long and hard to provide for us, then surely it must be here on the Isle of Wight. This is after all the 'Isle of UK' in microcosm!

Main picture **Ryde Esplanade:**
Running into Ryde Esplanade station in June 1966, Class 'O2' 0-4-4T No 20 *Shanklin* has the de rigeur rake of five coaches, as it passes the energetic souls walking from Pier to mainland alongside the railway and tramway. Ex-L&SWR 211, the loco came to the island in 1923, to assume the persona that would last the rest of its lifetime. Following the end of steam at the end of the year, No 20 was withdrawn officially on 18 January 1967. *Geoff King*

Below **Brading:** Another crossing of trains at Brading, but this time with a wider view of the surrounding hinterland. The incoming fireman again has the token ready for exchange and the waiting station staff member can just be seen at the foot of the shot. Class 'O2' 0-4-4T No 22 appropriately named *Brading*

approaches with a train from Ryde, whilst Class 'O2' 0-4-4T No 24 *Calbourne* waits for its turn to restart its train north. Coming to the island in 1924 and 1925 respectively – ex-L&SWR 215 and 209 – both were there at the end, but, whilst most of the remaining fleet were officially removed from stock on 18 January 1967,

somewhat strangely, No 24 was not withdrawn until 16 March. Happily, it was to be spared extinction, becoming the feature locomotive in preservation on the new Isle of Wight Railway. *Geoff King*

The first main route closures on the island took place on 15 September 1952 when the line from Merstone to Ventnor (West) succumbed. This was followed all too soon by the Newport - Freshwater route on 20 September 1953. Newport - Sandown was the next to go closing on 6 February 1956. This left just the Cowes - Newport - Smallbrook Junction and the Ryde - Shanklin - Ventnor lines. With the publication of the Beeching Report came the news that these remaining lines were earmarked for closure, save for the short stretch from Ryde Pier to St. Johns a distance of just over 1 mile. At its peak the island's railways extended to over 50 route miles. With the Southern Region of British Railways favouring electric traction and the demise of steam set to take place throughout the mainland network within just a few years decisions had to be taken in respect of the motive power and rolling stock on the island's railways.

The carriages were long in the tooth and the steam locomotives were increasingly difficult to maintain as the mainland infrastructure moved away from steam.

1968
THE END
40
OF STEAM
YEARS
2008

Below **Smallbrook Junction:** South of Ryde, Smallbrook Junction was the 'parting of the ways' for the erstwhile branch to Newport and Cowes and the main line to Ventnor. By the date of this view, in June 1966, the former had closed the previous February and the latter truncated to Shanklin in the April. In this distinctly rural view, an unidentified member of the island's small fleet restarts from signals. Railway preservationists have striven to recreate something of a railway presence, with Wootton station, on the old Newport line, opening in 1971 as a base. 20 years later, Smallbrook Junction station was opened in 1991 at the point where the Isle of Wight Steam Railway meets the current Island Line. It is only served on days that both the Island Line and the Steam Railway are open, as there is no access either by path or by road. *Geoff King*

In the event the line beyond St.Johns as far as Shanklin was saved and British Railways decided to electrify the line from Ryde Pier through to Shanklin using third rail and Ex-London Transport tube train stock. The line from Shanklin to Ventnor having closed on 18 April 1966, the last steam hauled service on the route ran on 31 December 1966 between Ryde Pier and Shanklin. The Island then entered a period when for the first time, passengers arriving on the Island would not be met by a train service, since 16 June 1862 when the first line, The Cowes & Newport Line, opened! This state of affairs lasted until 20 March 1967 when the 43 redundant London Transport tube vehicles entered service.

One of the most magnificent collections of historic railway vehicles to be seen on any heritage railway today can now be seen on **The Isle of Wight Steam Railway**. Passengers on the railway are virtually sure to be travelling in a carriage at least seventy five years old, the most modern carriage in regular service dating from 1924! Fortunately Six bogie carriages of London, Brighton and South Coast Railway and South Eastern and Chatham Railway origin

Main picture **Ryde Pier:** The sun shone brightly for our photographer on 13 September and has helped to create this picturesque view of a late afternoon train crossing from the Pier to the Esplanade. Five coaches might seem a tad excessive,

but such was the volume of traffic, even on the now truncated Shanklin-Ryde stretch, that they were often in danger of not actually being sufficient! Class 'O2' 0-4-4T No 20 *Shanklin* came to the island in 1923, having previously been No 211 in L&SWR stock. It lasted until the end of steam on the island and was scrapped sometime thereafter. *Frank Cassell*

Right **Ryde (Esplanade):** No 20 is again seen on the afternoon of 13 September, this time arriving in Esplanade station. The Indian Summer has helped bring out the shirt sleeves despite a breeze from the sea and there is a relaxed air about the scene that is absent from today's railways. With such a limited stock of motive power, the Works at Ryde had to be on top of their game to keep the locos running and some evidence of hard work can be seen on No 20's smokebox. *Frank Cassell*

were acquired by *The Wight Locomotive Society*, along with a variety of wagons, at the end of steam in 1966. After initial restoration at Newport Station, the move to Havenstreet and the establishment of the Isle of Wight Steam Railway in 1971, ensured a full restoration could be completed. Five of the original coaches are in regular service at the time of writing. In the early 1970s a plan was formulated to acquire grounded bodies of carriages which had been either built for or purchased second-hand by the old Island railway companies or had been imported to the Island by the Southern Railway, for eventual return to passenger service. Various underframes for use under these historic carriages have been acquired and, to date, four vehicles have been fully restored.

The tradition during the steam age was to name locomotives after the towns and villages on the Island and full details of the locomotives can be found on *pages 65 & 82*.

1968
THE END OF STEAM YEARS
2008

Inset below **Ryde:** The location at Ryde accommodated both engine shed and loco Works. The former is seen here, again on 13 September, as Class 'O2' 0-4-4T No14 *Fishbourne* has a moment of rest outside the shed between the

intensive schedules.
The station is to the right and the Works building beyond. Fishbourne was previously L&SWR 178 and came to the island in 1936. The shed building seen here was the third such facility at Ryde, opened in 1930 by the Southern Railway and replacing the two earlier ones provided by the Isle of Wight Railway. The earliest opened in 1864 and closed ten years later when it was incorporated into the Works complex; and the second was on the opposite, west side of St Johns station, a little to the south of the later construction. Closing in 1930 when the final shed was opened, it was subsequently demolished. The BR shed closed with the end of steam on 31 December 1966 and it, too, was then razed to the ground. *Frank Cassell*

Above **Seaton Junction:** The L&NWR branch to Luffenham ran like a tentacle from the 'octopus" centre at Rugby and, although it ran through sparse countryside and rural communities, with only Market Harborough being of any size, the running rights over Midland metals onwards from Luffenham gave the predominantly WCML Company a route through to Peterborough. Seaton Junction had importance, with branches to Uppingham and Peterborough and a regular service to/from Stamford. On 27 March 1965, a year before closure of the Seaton-Luffenham stretch, 'Standard' Class 2 2-6-2T No 84008 heads the 5.57 p.m. local to Stamford, passing under the ex-Midland route to Oakham, just north of Seaton.

Below **Near Stamford:** Another view two miles west of Stamford of 'Standard Class 2' 2-6-2T No 84008, as it heads the 2.50 p.m. shuttle from Seaton on 27 March 1965, proudly displaying its lined livery and the 'temporary' name *Sally* chalked on the tank side. Note the air pumps for the push-pull operation; and the variation of maroon liveries on the two non-corridor coaches, the leading one being the cleaner and graced with cantrail and bodyside stripes, together with what looks to be 'First Class' designation on the middle three doors. *Mike Mensing*

...We lost 1966

Many rural branch lines...

Left **Morcott Tunnel:** Morcott station was the first one out of Seaton on the short run to Stamford and, like its contemporaries, it closed in June 1966. A little over a year earlier, on Easter Monday, 19 April 1965, 'Standard' Class 2 2-6-2T No 84008 is again seen, this time at the north end of Morcott Tunnel, just south of the station, with the 12.38 p.m. shuttle to Stamford.

Right **Uppingham:** At the end of a branch line from Seaton, Uppingham railway station opened in 1894 and was located at the bottom of Queen Street. Passenger services were withdrawn in 1960 and the line closed completely in 1964. The station area has now been redeveloped as an industrial estate. Access to the short branch was by a spur mid-way between Seaton and Morcott. In this delightful colour portrait, the alignment of that spur can be seen striking out to the left of the front carriage. 'Standard' Class 2 2-6-2T No 84008 is again the motive power of the train but, contrary to appearances, it is in push-pull mode, approaching us with the 1.28 p.m. train from Stamford on 19 April 1965. *All Mike Mensing*

8

Left **Stamford:** The eastern 'terminus' of the shuttle train. On a dull, misty morning, Class 2 2-6-2T No 41219 has arrived at Stamford with its load of commuters, as the 8.15 a.m. from Seaton. The grandeur of the station buildings – and where else would the 'Gents' be so well designed!? – is historic and has led to them being granted Grade 2 Listed status; and even today's railways are not wholly ignorant of public relations and the need for upkeep of properties, as a £500,000 programme to clean up the town's historic station was announced by Network Rail in September 2007.

After the massive number of closures following the Beeching Report and the fact that BR had a deficit of £132m for 1965, it was perhaps inevitable that closures would continue, but some slight comfort nevertheless was had in that the number in 1966 should show a reduction to the previous year – 266 against 308. However, this did not prevent major lines seeing closure during the year, not least the Somerset & Dorset and Great Central railways and the eradication of steam from the Isle of Wight. All three are featured in this section of our examination of steam's nemesis. In addition, BR's plans were to eliminate steam working in Scotland by the end of the year.

By the end of 1965, Scotland had 404 steam locomotives on its books, (out of a total of 2,987 throughout the UK), spread through 22 sheds, but so many of the routes over which they might have found employ were already operated by diesels, either locomotives or multiple units. The whole of the Great North of Scotland and Highland railways were totally dieselised motive power, along with the West Highland line to Mallaig and Fort William and the former Caledonian section between Crianlarich and Oban. Edinburgh-Aberdeen via Dundee, Glasgow-Aberdeen and Dundee (via Perth) were similarly handled, with the one major exception being the 3-hr inter-city service between Glasgow and Aberdeen that was partly hauled by 'A4s'. Virtually all inter-regional services were diesel operated and the vast majority of the erstwhile steam hauled local services were now in the hands of DMUs. Depots, too, like Haymarket were being converted to diesel fare, or else were closed.

Of the eight 'A4s' that began the year, only three survived as far as late summer – No 60019 *Bittern*, No 60024 *Kingfisher* and No 60034 *Lord Faringdon* – all going 'en bloc' on 24 September from Aberdeen (Ferryhill) shed. The sole remaining 'A3' – No 60052 *Prince Palatine* – just made it into the following year, before being withdrawn by St Margaret's shed on 29 January, although it had actually been out of steam since December with boiler problems. Of other express locomotives, the three extant 'A2s' – No

Left **Minehead:** A link with the past at Minehead Station on the West Somerset Railway is this Walter Macfarlane & Co No 5 Drinking Fountain manufactured in the company's Saracen Foundry in c1883 fully restored by the WSR to be enjoyed as it would have been back in 1966. *MJS*

60528 *Tudor Minstrel*, No 60530 *Sayajirao* and No 60532 *Blue Peter* – went progressively in June, November and, finally, 31 December. The first and last from Ferryhill and 60530 from Dundee. During the year, No 60007 *Sir Nigel Gresley* was saved from scrap by the 'A4 Preservation Society'.

The largest single class on the ScR at the turn of the year was Stanier's 'Black 5', of which there were 90 nominally in operation; with the balance made up of 14 different classes. By comparison, there were 328 main line and 318 shunting diesels, 191 DMU sets and 91 EMU sets – the latter at Hyndland depot for Stage 1 of the expanding suburban electric service.

As in previous – and seemingly, every – years, prices were increased by BR, with freight specifically increasing by 5% and even the humble buffet being affected. Tea was to rise from 6d to 7d (14%!) and coffee to 1/- from 10d (20%)!

January 1 saw 46115 *Scots Guardsman* arrive at Carlisle on its last working. Returning to Kingmoor shed, it was immediately withdrawn, thus bringing the 'Royal Scots' to extinction as a class. January 3 saw several ER depots and stations transferred to MR jurisdiction by boundary changes. Lines affected included Nottingham (Victoria)-Grantham/Newark Castle and the steam shed and marshalling yard at Colwick. The same date also saw the closure of the long-after lamented Cheltenham (St James) station, with all traffic in the town then handled through the ex-LMS Lansdown station, which did have the benefit of being on a main through line, but was further from the town centre. By contrast, a new station was opened at Garston, on the Watford Junction-St Albans Abbey branch on 7 February. A simple, unstaffed halt, it was served by a two-car DMU set. Five days later, a 'Blue Pullman' was used on a football special from Walsall to Norwich Thorpe, being the first visit of the type to Norwich; and on 5 March a similar working took fans from Coventry to Liverpool Lime Street. Four days after this last date, three nameplates from Bullied 'Pacifics' – *Dorchester* (ex-34042), *Cunard White Star* (35004) and *Canadian Pacific* (35005) – were presented to the Canadian Railroad Historical Association for display in the National Railway Museum, Delson, Quebec.

April 18 saw the inauguration of main line electrified services between Euston, Crewe, Liverpool and Manchester, with it being trumpeted as an opportunity for the London Midland Region of BR to show just how good and efficient rail travel could be! New Pullman coaches for these routes had been introduced in January, built at Derby Works and painted in grey with blue at window level. As if aware of the competition, the ECML introduced an improved timetable on the same day, with regular-interval services throughout the day, waiting times at stations reduced and acceleration of up to 20 minutes in trains to the northeast and Scotland; and the MML did not wish to be overshadowed, with its own revised timetables from that date, a more intensive use of the fleet of diesel locomotives and fast, frequent and regular trains between St Pancras, the East Midlands and the North. April 18 also saw the WR introduce its first 100-mph trains between Paddington and Bristol, with over 60 miles of track having been relaid in preparation. In the new blue and grey livery, they were double-headed, with a combined output of 3,500 hp.

On 6 April, 46416 achieved some notoriety when it 'ran away' for the second time! When still fairly new, it over-ran buffer stops at Castleton sidings and fell 20ft into a Rochdale street (!), but on this day in 1966 it escaped down a siding alongside the former Bacup branch. It buried itself in six condemned wagons that stood in the siding, resulting in its chimney and safety valves being ripped off! Additional serious boiler damage saw it instantly condemned!

During the year another record was achieved, but not an enviable one! The last remaining stretches of double track on the ex-Cambrian line between Shrewsbury and Aberystwyth – the 4½ miles from Welshpool to Forden and the mile-long Llanbadarn Crossing-Aberystwyth – brought into being, at 115 miles, the longest single-track stretch on the Midland Region! 1966 also saw the demise of the unique English Electric 4-6-0 gas-turbine locomotive GT3, at Thos. W Ward Ltd's scrapyard in Salford. Built in 1961 and bearing a striking resemblance to a steam locomotive, it ran only 11,104 miles, including a period on the ex-GCR. Little is known of its capital expenditure, performances or economics, but it would seem that BR did not deem the experiment a success!

The summer saw 169 locomotives at Dai Woodham's scrapyard at Barry; 'Coronation' Class 4-6-2 No 46235 *City of Birmingham* presented by BR to the City of Birmingham Science Museum; No 'D49' Class 4-4-0 No 62712 *Morayshire* to the Royal Scottish Museum; the Glasgow Museum of Transport receive six ancient locomotives; 'Jubilee' Class 4-6-0 No 45596 *Bahamas* saved from scrap; the BRB increasingly concerned at the losses of around £1,000 per week by the museums at Swindon, Clapham and York; the opening of a new terminal at Kensington (Olympia) for BR's 'Motorail' services, providing a spacious passenger lounge and a buffet catering for family needs, thus becoming the World's first all-line car-train terminal; Immingham diesel depot

opened; and the opening of a Freightliner terminal at Garston, near Liverpool, built on the site of a former freight depot. Sadly, in the opposite direction, Beyer Peacock's Gorton Foundry closed after 111years; and remaining freight trains were withdrawn from the Northampton-Wellingborough route.

1966 LINE CLOSURES - A Selection

Date	From	To	Passenger/Goods
London Midland Region			
3 January	Lancaster	Morecambe	*Passenger*
	Morecambe	Heysham	*Passenger*
10 January	Leighton Buzzard	Dunstable North	*Closed*
18 April	Crewe	Chester General	*Local Passenger*
	Keswick	Workington	*Closed*
2 May	Desford	Leicester WB	*Closed*
6 June	Melton Mowbray	Nottingham Midland	*Closed*
	Rugby Midland	Peterborough	*Passenger*
	Seaton Junction	Stamford	*Closed*
5 September	Aylesbury	Rugby Central	*Passenger*
	Banbury	Woodford Halse	*Closed*
	Nottingham Vict.	Sheffield Victoria	*Passenger*
5 December	Verney Junction	Buckingham	*Closed*
Southern Region			
21 February	Ryde Pier	Cowes	*Closed*
7 March	Templecombe	Poole	*Closed*
	Salisbury	Exeter	*Local Passenger*
18 April	Shanklin	Ventnor	*Closed*
Scottish Region			
28 February	Aberdeen (Ferryhill Jnc)	Ballater	*Passenger*
27 June	Paisley (Gilmour St.)	Dalry (Brownhill Jnc)	*Passenger*
North Eastern Region			
30 November	Church Fenton	Tadcaster	*Closed*
19 December	Morley	Leeds (City)	*Passenger*
Eastern Region			
7 November	Cambridge	Bury St Edmunds	*Local Passenger*
Western Region			
7 March	Bath Green Park	Templecombe	*Closed*
	Bath Green Park	Mangotsfield	*Passenger*
	Evercreech Jnc	Highbridge/Burnham	*Passenger*
18 April	Newbury	Westbury	*Local Passenger*
1 June	Stonehouse	Nailsworth	*Closed*
3 October	Taunton	Barnstaple Jnc	*Closed*
	Yatton	Clevedon	*Closed*
	Yeovil Jnc	Yeovil	*Closed*
7 November	Gobowen	Oswestry	*Passenger*

Locoshed closures by region

1966 SHED CLOSURES

Date	Code	Name	Steam/Closed
3 January	1B	Camden	Closed
6 June	2B	Nuneaton	Closed
18 April	6B	Mold Junction	Closed
3 October	6G	Llandudno Junction	Closed
5 December	6J	Hollyhead	Steam
12 December	12B	Upperby	Steam
12 December	12E	Barrow	Steam
13 June	15A	Wellingborough	Steam
13 June	15C	Leicester	Steam
3 October	16B	Kirkby-in-Ashfield	Steam
3 January	16D	Annesley	Closed
? September	17B	Burton	Closed
3 October	18B	Westhouses	Steam
28 March	21B	Bescot	Closed
14 February	24D	Lower Darwen	Closed
14 February	24F	Fleetwood	Closed
18 April	24J	Lancaster	Closed
22 October	26B	Agecroft	Closed
22 October	27A	Bank Hall	Closed
6 June	27C	Southport	Closed
? May	36A	Doncaster	Steam
26 February	36C	Frodingham	Steam
? February	40B	Immingham	Steam
12 December	40E	Colwick	Steam
6 February	41J	Langwith Junction	Closed
27 March	51A	Darlington	Closed
19 June	52D	Tweedmouth	Closed
28 February	52E	Percy Main	Steam
? November	55C	Farnley Junction	Closed
6 November	55D	Royston	Closed
12 June	55H	Neville Hill	Steam
29 August	64F	Bathgate	Closed
3 January	64G	Hawick	Closed
? November	65A	Eastfield	Steam
7 November	65B	St. Rollox	Closed
13 June	65J	Stirling	Closed
26 November	66D	Greenock	Closed
6 October	67B	Hurlford	Closed
3 October	67C	Ayr	Steam

London Midland Region
Eastern Region
North Eastern Region
Scottish Region
Southern Region
Western Region

1966 SHED CLOSURES

Date	Code	Name	Steam/Closed
1 May	67E	Dumfries	Closed
? October	67F	Stranraer	Closed
31 December	70H	Ryde	Closed
3 January	81C	Southall	Steam
3 January	81F	Oxford	Closed
7 March	82F	Bath Green Park	Closed
? March	82G	Templecombe	Closed
3 October	84C	Banbury	Closed
7 November	84E	Tyseley	Steam
11 July	84F	Stourbridge Jct	Closed
1 January	85B	Gloucester HR	Steam
5 December	89C	Machynlleth	Steam

As the year wore on, there came a realisation that the draconian measures of the Beeching Report were, perhaps, not the answer. In the year's Transport White Paper, a statement that "commercial viability is important but secondary" seemed to indicate a change of heart by the Government and acceptance of a need for a rethink. The current deficit of BR was to be absorbed by Government and closure proposals reassessed, leaving a system substantially larger than envisaged by under Beeching. A new national freight organisation was to be constructed, with a review of road haulage licensing and comparisons between the cost of the existing railway and any replacement thereof, and then a call for BR to increase efficiency and productivity; and a new station was opened at Billingham.

Following the closure of the GCR through route, the York-Bournemouth-Poole cross-country services were redirected via Derby and Birmingham, excluding the previous important stops at Nottingham, Loughborough, Leicester, Rugby and Banbury. 5 November saw the last public run by a Class 'V2' 2-6-2, when No 60836 hauled a special excursion from Edinburgh Waverley to Aberdeen, via Perth.

List of Isle of Wight locomotives carrying Island place names

With the exception of some of the earliest locomotives used by the Isle of Wight Central Railway, Island town and village names have traditionally been used to name Islandbased locomotives. The majority of the names used were of places directly associated with the railway; however, Bonchurch, Chale, Osborne, Seaview, Shorwell and Totland were remote from the railway system, and Fishbourne's association was only through the ferry service. This table shows the specific use of these local names over the years; it should be noted that in a few cases the locomotives listed did not always carry both the name and the associated number at the same time,

Name	Class	Number	To Island	Disposal
Ashey	Adams '02' 0-4-4	W28	1926	Scrapped 1967
Alverstone	Adams '02' 0-4-4	W29	1926	Scrapped 1966
Bembridge	Manning Wardle 0-6-0	-	1882	War Service
	Stroudley 'Alx' 0-6-0	W4 then W14	1929	To mainland 1936
	Adams '02' 0-4-4	W33	1936	Scrapped 1967
Bonchurch	Beyer Peacock 2-4-0	W18	1883	Scrapped 1928
	Adams '02' 0-4-4	W32	1928	Scrapped 1965
Brading	Beyer Peacock 2-4-0	Not Numbered / W17	1876(?)	It is possible that this loco could have been used on the Island by contractors from 1863 to 1872, later to become St Helens. Scrapped 1926
	Adams '02' 0-4-4	W22	1924	Scrapped 1926
Carisbrooke	Stroudley 'Alx' 0-6-0	W3 then W13	1927	To mainland 1949
	Adams '02' 0-4-4	W36	1949	Scrapped 1967
Calbourne	Adams '02' 0-4-4	W24	1925	To IWSR 1967
Chale	Adams '02' 0-4-4	W31	1927	Scrapped 1967
Cowes	Beyer Peacock 2-4-0	IWC4	1876	Scrapped 1925

Table continues on Page 82

STEAM ENDS AT
OXFORD
Motive Power Depot

**Brian Grant remembers...
The transition from Steam locomotives to Diesel and Electric locomotives**

"Little did I realise on my first journey to Salisbury Motive Power Depot in September 1952 that I was going to play a part in the biggest changes faced by the railway industry. Salisbury MPD had an allocation of over seventy steam locomotives in 1952 but within fifteen years the depot would be closed and the majority of locomotives consigned to the scrap heap. Fortunately some of the locomotives that had been allocated to Salisbury have joined the list of preserved locomotives. Leaving Salisbury in August 1961 I moved to Bricklayer's Arms where steam was to be eliminated within five months. A further move to Dover in December 1962 took me into the new era for Motive Power. It was then time to move backwards to Southall where a fleet of steam locomotives, in a poor condition, were still working freight services and where necessary used to replace failed Diesel locomotives. Southall was also the dumping ground for condemned steam locomotives. A further move to Oxford in late 1965 saw the end of steam motive power at that depot marked on January 3 1966 with the last steam locomotive hauled north-bound Pines Express. All that remained for my memories of steam haulage was to have one final footplate trip in March 1967 from Waterloo to Bournemouth."

Left **OXFORD MPD 3 January 1966:** 'Hall' Class 4-6-0 No 6998 *Burton Agnes Hall,* The rostered loco for the last steam hauled *Pines Express,* and last steam hauled service from the city, prepares to leave Oxford MPD. The Lord Mayor of Oxford, Mrs Florence Kathleen Lower is on the Footplate with Reggie Hanks while those with their feet firmly on the ground are *left to right* David Pattisson, Joe Trethewey, Bill Sidwell, Albert Barnes; and Area Maintenance Engineer. *Brian Grant.*

Left inset **OXFORD MPD:** Standing in front of the *Burton Agnes Hall* 'name plate' are *left to right* Right: Joe Trethewey, unknown, unknown, unknown, Brian Grant, Hamwell Williams (Chairman of Loco Departmental Committee (LDC), Tom Simmons (Secretary of LDC) and Bill Miles (?). The ' name & number plates' were not what they appear as by this time the original plates had long since been removed and the ones seen here were fashioned from plywood by a 'wizard at Oxford MPD specially for the occasion! The MPD closed to steam the same day. *Brian Grant*

Right **London (Waterloo):** The sort of photographic access – and cheeky smile – that you would only find with steam! With dog-end glued to his lips, the driver of 'Standard' Class 4 2-6-0 No 76026 handling LCGB's 'The Dorset Coast Express' grins for the camera during a pause at Wareham on 7 May 1967. Having been on the rear of the tour from Wareham to Swanage, top-and-tailing with 'West Country' Class 4-6-2 No 34023 *Blackmore Vale* – known as *Blackmoor Vale* for the first four years of its life – No 76026 had headed the special back up the branch to the main line, where it was detached for it to make its way to Weymouth for duty on the tour later on. Seen around 2.30 p.m., the tour was on time and loco and tour would meet again in two hours time, ready for the 5.00 p.m. departure from Weymouth for Bournemouth, double-headed with 'Standard' Class 5 4-6-0 No 73029.

Right One of the delights of our photographer was to capture the human face of the railways. Away from the metropolis for a change, we are treated to a sight so common over the years that most travellers paid it little attention. On 6 June 1967, the Basingstoke Guard waves his flag to give the all clear for the onward transmission of the 7.05 a.m. from his home station out of Farnborough, in the last week of steam for this service.

Below **London (Waterloo):** We are still a few days short of the very end, but the forthcoming event is being widely advertised on the side of the tank – "July 10th – End of SR Steam". On 29 June, 'Standard' Class 3 2-6-2T No 82019's fireman has replenished the tanks while his mate, Driver Hurley of Nine Elms, chats to one of the porters at Waterloo. New on 7 October 1952, No 82019's first duties were 'out west' at Exmouth Junction shed. There for ten years, a move east took it to Eastleigh on 24 September 1962, from where it travelled 'to the smoke' two months later. Thence shedded at Nine Elms, it shuttled in and out of Waterloo until final withdrawal after the end of steam there, without any reprieve of a despatch to pastures new.

1968
THE END
OF STEAM
YEARS
2008

1967

Farewell to Southern Region Steam

As with the previous year, the number of closures for lines, junctions, etc. again reduced – this time from 266 to 220 – but that was progressive during the year. One major change, however, for the areas covered, came into play on 1 January, when the erstwhile Eastern and North Eastern Regions of BR were merged into one Eastern Region, with headquarters in York and to hopefully save administrative costs of around £1.6m per year! G F Fiennes was the new General Manager. That date also signalled the end of planned steam locomotive repairs at BR Works and on 2 February, 'Britannia' Class 4-6-2 No 70013 *Oliver Cromwell* had the honour of the being the last out of Crewe. All future repairs and/or maintenance duties were to be from local depots. The announcement was also made at this time to discontinue all-steam hauled specials; and to eliminate steam from BR by the end of the year, with the possible exception of the northwest. Announcements were also made affecting Pullman services. Those out of Euston were to be accelerated from 6 March; WR services were to be expanded; and the sets were to receive yellow front-end warning panels! 1967 also saw the emergence of larger yellow panels on Locomotives, covering most of the front ends.

Below **London (Waterloo):** We are again with the 7.05 a.m. from Basingstoke, but this time three days later, on 9 June – the last day of steam for this train. 'West Country' Class 4-6-2 No 34024 *Tamar Valley* has the honours and is here on the very last few yards into Waterloo station, for the 8.00 a.m. arrival and the commuters to rush off to their desks! The 'future' stands ahead, in the guise of EMUs and a 'Class 47' diesel. New in 1946 and initially numbered 21C124 by Bullied, No 34024 was a very 'loyal' loco, working from Exmouth Junction for most of its life, up until 11 November 1963. Thereafter, only one other shed had its service – Bournemouth, from where it bowed out on 9 July 1967, together with steam on BR(SR).

Another milestone was reached on 6 January, when the 1,000th diesel locomotive to be completed at Derby emerged from the Works. D7667 was resplendent in the new BR loco livery of all over blue with white numbers and double-arrow symbol and the all-yellow front end. Special commemorative plaques were fitted to the sides before despatch to the southern end of the WCML, officially allocated to 'D01', signifying the Willesden area. 1 March was an electrifying day for the Isle of Wight's railways, when the power was switched on over the 8½-mile stretch between Ryde Pier Head and Shanklin. 6 March was similarly eventful, as it saw the introduction of a new timetable bringing electrification to Birmingham (New Street) and services to and from the Capital; and April Fool's Day was one of excitement, with the re-opening of the Isle of Man Railway. In 1949, BR owned and employed around 8,000 horses

Above **London (Waterloo):** Things do not always run smoothly! Whilst steam lovers may home in on the 'West Country' Pacific on the far side of Waterloo, the more astute may notice that the EMU on the right is off the rails! So near and yet so far, the 4-EPB 5129 was entering the platform on a train from Guildford when the rear end decided to go elsewhere! Gangers and engineering staff are gathered but not, apparently, focused on where to place their attention. A position so different to what would be the situation in the 21st century, when the RAIB and H&S authorities would have their fingers on the pulse – and hi-vis vests and BTP officers would be all over the place! For those interested, 'West Country' Class 4-6-2 34104 *Bere Alston* is about to leave with the 10.30 a.m. express to Bournemouth and Weymouth on 28 March 1967. In the centre are EMUs from Bournemouth and to Portsmouth.

Right **London (Waterloo):** We are making progress! Moments later and steam has come to the rescue of the EPB. 41298 has backed up to the errant EMU and is about to assist the re-railing and movement of the set to the sidings for further inspection. New on 3 November 1951, Class '2' 2-6-2T No 41298 was a BR(SR) throughout its life, in London at the start and end of things, but elsewhere in between. Allocated to Nine Elms when pressed into service this day, it was another loco to survive to the end of steam on the SR and to be withdrawn immediately afterwards.

throughout the system but this number was down to just one by 1967 and in the early part of the year that last one, a 24-yr old bay and white carthorse called 'Charlie', was retired from shunting horseboxes containing racehorses at Newmarket.

Our railways have never been and can never be 100% safe; but, thankfully, there are few people killed each year compared to the vast numbers travelling. However, on 28 February, nine died and eleven were injured, when the 13.15 EMU train from Manchester to Coventry ran into a diesel shunter at Stechford station, becoming derailed and the first two coaches overturned, damaging the track and bringing down the overhead wires. Less than a week later, on 5 March, the 22.30 King's Cross-Edinburgh expressed derailed at Conington. The 11-coach train, hauled by 'Deltic' D9004 *Queen's Own Highlander*, included sleeping cars and three TPO vehicles and was reported to be travelling at 85mph at the time of the accident. Five passengers died in the overturned coaches.

As well as ushering in the new electrified service at Birmingham (see above) and dispensing with numerous stations throughout the UK (see partial list on page 80), 6 March was also notable for the disappearance of the *Cambrian Coast Express* – 'Standard' Class 4-6-0 No 75033 hauling the last up service – *The Pines Express* and the Birmingham (Snow Hill)-Birkenhead through trains; and for passengers being able to buy their tickets by credit card for the first time, using Barclaycard at Birmingham (new Street), Newcastle and Leeds. Fourteen days later, the electrified Isle of Wight opened for business.

In the spring of 1967, the Government published a map, jointly with the BRB, of the envisaged network of railways in the UK. Whilst it was recognised that there could still be closures, the basic premise had shifted to one of showing

"the stabilised network planned to meet social as well as economic and commercial needs." At around 11,000 miles, this showed a system vastly different to one that would have pertained if the Beeching plans and their aftermath had been continued; and it included "certain lines essential to the life of remote areas." It also recognised that the future of freight lines would need to be reconsidered. In addition, the Government had identified services that were important to the life of the community but which could not cover their costs and the BRB would be relieved of the burden for these. This was the third announcement in four years – this latest under a Labour administration – and showed that some common sense had fought its way back into railway planning. Some of the places that thus were granted a reprieve from the draconian Beeching Plan included Wick and Thurso; Dumfries; Scarborough; Blaenau Ffestiniog; Aberystwyth; Oxford-Worcester; Salisbury-Exeter; Penzance; Skegness and Lowestoft. 3 April saw the introduction of a new, direct, high-capacity container service between Camden Freight Depot in London and Belfast, via Heysham, using Freightliner containers and wagons; the end for BR's last steam operated branch line, from Brockenhurst and Lymington Pier – with Class '2' 2-6-2T No 41312 working the last such service; and from the same day, some Waterloo-Bournemouth services were scheduled for electric operation, with an up-grade in speeds. They went totally electric from 10 July, along with trains to Southampton and a push-pull service between Bournemouth and Weymouth.

Railway preservation was gaining increasing popularity, with several locomotives reaching the safety of private hands during the year – such as Class '2' 2-6-2T No 41241 and Class '1F' 0-6-0T No 41708 at the K&WVR and 'A4' Class 4-6-2 No 60009 *Union of South Africa* to a group of business associates headed by John Cameron – and, on 15 April,

BARNSTAPLE JUNCTION

ENDANGERED SIGNS

STATION NAME BOARDS

THE END OF STEAM

Left: **Barnstaple Junction** A remnant from the days of steam was captured in the late 1970s on the platform at this far flung outpost of the Southern Region, certainly endangered as the Beeching Axe swept away stations, Name Boards are now much sought after and Totems change hands for thousands of pounds at auction.

1967, less than a fortnight from the final curtain, whilst No 41312 takes empty stock towards Waterloo, as the 6.23 p.m. from Clapham Yard, to position it in a platform to become the 6.54 p.m. semi-fast to Basingstoke. New towards the end of August 1949, *Saunton* spent the first half of its life at Bournemouth shed, before moving to Nine Elms on 6 June 1958 and then Eastleigh in September 1964. It has just nine days of life left but is still on top-link rosters.

Below **Between Clapham Junction and Waterloo:** Whilst lineside shots have their own power and drama, head-on views of closing trains add that certain *je ne sais quoi!* On the 'open road' between Clapham Junction and Waterloo, 'West Country' Class No 34093 *Saunton* is accelerating out of the capital and is about to pass Class '2' 2-6-2T 41312 heading inwards. The 'West Country' Pacific heads the 6.23 p.m. Relief Waterloo-Bournemouth express on 30 June

The Corris Society was inaugurated, joining the expanding throng of enthusiasts determined to save as much of our railways as they could. Negotiations were ongoing with the owner of the ex-Corris railway building at Machynlleth, with the intention of turning it into a museum, but these were to prove fruitless. Meanwhile, other locos made longer journeys, with 'Schools' Class 4-4-0 No 30926 *Repton* and 'M7' Class 0-4-4T No 30053 being moved to Liverpool Gladstone Dock on 18 April, for transhipment to Steamtown Foundation, Bellows Falls, Vermont, Virginia, USA; and 'A4' Class 4-6-2 No 60010 *Dominion of Canada* found its way to the Canadian Railroad Historical Association, near Montreal.

The last two steam engines still working in Scotland a pair of 'J36' Class 0-6-0s were withdrawn in June – No 65288 from Dunfermline on 24th and No 65345 from Thornton Junction on the same day – and they were reputedly the oldest working locomtioves on BR. The July 1967 issue of *Railway Magazine* celebrated 70 years of railway publishing – but in typical low key style prevalent of those halcyon days, unlike what would now be a major trumpeting exercise; and in that same issue, it was announced that BR was looking ahead to closure of the Settle-Carlisle route after the completion of WCML, estimated to be around 1970/71! And the end of steam on the Southern Region came on 9 July. The following day, 201 locos were noted at Barry, awaiting their fate. The end of the month witnessed another accident, when English Electric prototype 'DP2' was in collision with the Cliffe-Uddingston block cement train at Coldbeck in Yorkshire. Seven passengers were killed and 45 injured, although both driver and secondman were miraculously unhurt! Barbara Castle also announced during the month that BR was not about to sell the VoR line out of

MEN OF SOUTHERN STEAM
FIREMAN
THE END OF STEAM

Above **London (Waterloo):** Another human portrait. Seemingly a little perplexed at his photograph being taken, the fireman of Class '2' 2-6-2T No 41298 fixes his stare on the camera, whilst his driver is unconcerned. The loco had brought the empty stock into Waterloo on 5 April 1967 for it to be an outgoing 'Bournemouth Belle'. Having filled its coaches with travellers and reached the appointed time, the guard has signalled 'right away' and the 'Belle' has just begun to move forward on its long journey.

Below **London (Waterloo):** More empty stock workings, but this time captured at Clapham Junction station. On 30 June 1967, 'Standard' Class 3 2-6-2T No 82019 moves away from its holding siding and begins the short journey to Waterloo, as Class '2' 2-6-2T No 41312 waits for its turn. Happily No 41312 was survive beyond withdrawal, to see preservation, but No 82019 was, like all the rest of the Class, not so lucky. A Southern loco the whole of its existence, it emerged from its birthplace on 7 October 1952, moving to Exmouth Junction shed. Eastleigh beckoned in September 1962 but, two months later, Nine Elms laid claim, for just such duties as seen here and this was to be its last move. Like others seen in these pages, survival was to the end of steam on BR(SR) but no further.

Above **Eastleigh:** A fitter on the railway was one of the unsung heroes. Often given difficult tasks, to keep the locos running, not infrequently in short time deadlines, with loco parts unyielding and the work dirty, cold and unappreciated, these men were a special breed, seemingly ever cheerful despite it all! One of their number is seen here at Eastleigh, working on 'Standard' Class 4 No 80016 on 4 June 1967. Make do and mend it so often was, particularly in these final months, but the public owed them a huge debt of gratitude.

Above right: No matter how hard the timetabling teams tried, there were always occasions when locomotives were in the wrong place! This could have been due to an imbalance in workings, loco failures, change of shed allocations, a trip to Works, or

any number of emergencies. Often the light engines would scuttle along main lines, anxious to avoid interrupting the important work of moving passengers or freight and, no doubt, Thomas would say, "They always seem in a hurry!". Here, 'West Country' Class 4-6-2

No 34102 *Lapford* epitomises the hurried appearance as it heads west on 5 July 1967, as seen from an empty EMU on a driver-training trip to London. Evidence that it is within days of the end is the absence of its nameplate on the boiler air casing.

Below **Between Millbrook and Southampton Central:** In common with what we have already seen around the UK, steam on BR(SR) did not all finish in one 'big bang'. Various services ended, piecemeal throughout

SOUTH EASTERN & CHATHAM RAILWAY
NOTICE
~TO~
CABDRIVERS.
Any Cabman skylarking or otherwise misconducting himself while on the Managing Committee's premises or Smoking whilst his Cab is standing alongside the Platform will be required to leave the Station immediately.

Aberystwyth; and on 30th, BR's last independent power station, at Stonebridge Park, between Euston and Watford, was closed down, with all future needs coming from the National Grid.

On 7 August, the Ministry of Transport announced a social cost/benefit study for the Machynlleth-Pwllheli section of the erstwhile Cambrian Railway – at about the same time as Caernarvonshire County Education Committee decided to continue with their £1,000 annual subsidy for school trains on the route! August also saw the opening of Willesden Freightliner Terminal, utilising two massive 'Goliath' cranes; and the final stages of construction at Brush's Flacon Works in Loughborough of the prototype single-engine 4,000hp Co-Co diesel, *Kestrel*. The first of the new 2,700hp Co-Cos for the WCML – later to become BR 'Class 50s' – were taking shape at Vulcan Works, Newton-le-Willows at the same time.

With the closure of the Perth-Forfar line on 4 September, BR made plans to base all future services to/from Perth station in the eastern, Dundee section, abandoning the rest of the facility and proposing to reduce this once mighty station to a very poor shadow of its former glory; and bearing in mind the refurbishment of 2007, it is interesting to note BR's proposals at this time to close St Pancras station and run a semi-fast service to Leicester from Moorgate Metropolitan station! Another decision that was not progressed was the proposal to withdraw passenger services over the Central Wales line, from Craven Arms to Llanelli. Elsewhere, demolition of the damaged Severn Bridge was begun.

the days and weeks before the final weekend in July 1967. One such service to go over to other forms of motive power was a regular running bullion special from Southampton Docks to Waterloo and the very last one of these steam hauled is seen on 3 July. With a mix of semi-detached and terraced housing as backdrop, 'West Country' Class No 34036 *Westward Ho* is itself patently near the end, with a painted smokebox number and shedplate and devoid of nameplate, as it heads for London with its short rake of bullion vans between Millbrook and Southampton Central. Originally number 21C136, it had initially been a Brighton district loco but made the long trip west, to Plymouth (Friary) in December 1950. Thereafter, it gradually moved back east through a variety of sheds, before ending up, with so many of its contemporaries, at Nine Elms and withdrawal with the end of steam on the Region.

Right **Guildford Shed:** Shed visits have long been a draw for enthusiasts, coming to worship at the Mecca that holds a number of idols in close proximity. It was a way of 'being up close and personal' with the objects of our desires. Even to the end when, by the reduction in steam rosters and a progressive standardisation over many years, there were still locos there to see and still with some variety between and among them. The date is 7 July 1967 and there is less than 48 hours to go for Guildford shed and for steam on the SR system. 'Standard' Class 5 4-6-0 No 73118 *King Leodegrance* and 'Standard' Class 4 2-6-0 No 76067 seem as if in conversation, surmising on future developments, with the latter wearing an impromptu inscription, "Farewell to steam – Last of the greats." Smoke still drifts lazily from No 76067's chimney, but it rather looks as though its neighbour, the 'Standard 5' has had its fire dropped.

As the year was drawing to a close, another piece of railway history was being consigned to the past, following an agreement between the BRB and NUR to dispense with brakevans on fully-fitted freight trains; double track was re-instated between Yeovil Junction and Sherborne, on the Salisbury-Exeter line, a little more than six months after it had been singled!; 26 October saw the end of another 'tradition', with the replacement by Freightliner containers on the erstwhile 'Condor' Glasgow-England freight runs, that had been introduced in 1959 and ran for some time behind the infamous 'Metrovik' diesels.

Following the announcement by BR of their intention to eliminate steam from its books by 5 August 1968, moves continued to remove as much as possible in as short a time span as could be achieved. Now corralled into the northwest, the final remnants of steam operation were being attacked on all fronts.

MEN OF SOUTHERN STEAM
FIREMAN
THE END OF STEAM

Below **Southampton:** We are back in Southampton, on 6 July, to see 'Battle of Britain' Class 4-6-2 No 34087 *145 Squadron* approaching Central station with the 11.25 a.m. from Weymouth, due shortly after 1 p.m.. Again the nameplate is missing and the general demeanour of the front-line, express locomotive leaves a lot to be desired. Fresh from Brighton Works on 31 January

1949, its first home was at Ramsgate shed. The stay there was short, however, before a move to the other end of the line, to Stewarts Lane on 12 May 1951. A mere two weeks later saw it then switch allegiance to Nine Elms, where it stayed until 14 September 1964 and a move to Eastleigh and the shed that was its home when seen here.

Above **Clapham Yard:** More portraits, though sadly without names recorded. Mixed duties and grades are represented by the sextet standing by Class '2' 2-6-2T No 41298 in Clapham Yard on 7 July 1967.

Above **Kensington (Olympia)** Another 'cheeky chappie'! With what appears to be a reverse turban, he leans on the cabsheet of Class '2' 2-6-2T No 41312 at Kensington (Olympia) on 30 June 1967, before preparing to assist his mate, Driver Walker, with the 5.06 p.m. departure to Clapham Junction.

In the last weeks of the year, steam was eradicated from sheds 8B (Warrington Dallam), 55A (Leeds Holbeck) and 56F (Low Moor) w.e.f. 2 October; 5B (Crewe South) and 8H (Birkenhead — where 42 steam locomotives were noted just two months earlier) from 6 November; and 8F (Wigan Springs Branch) and 8G (Sutton Oak) from 4 December. The last two closed completely.

Steam haulage of iron ore from Bidston Dock to John Summers & Sons Ltd steelworks at Shotton ended on 6 November, with the last trip being eleven bogie hopper wagons hauled by '9F' Class 2-10-0 No 92203. The loco was 'driven' by Sir Richard Summers, Director of the Company and a former Director of the LMS. Subsequently preserved by David Shepherd and named *Black Prince*, the loco was to recreate some of this in a photo shoot at Shotton steelworks some 30+ years later! 18 November saw Class '2' 2-6-0 No 46441 at Carnforth shed, painted in maroon livery and now in private ownership.

Right **London (Waterloo):** The last day and the very last steam hauled boat express from Southampton Docks has reached the buffer stops in London. Accompanied by a phalanx of adoring and/or mourning enthusiasts – and some who 'just wanted to be there'! – with a good collection of shirts and ties (!), 'West Country' Class 4-6-2 No 34021 *Dartmoor* – again without nameplate but at least with a 'genuine' front numberplate – lets off steam at Waterloo for the last time on 9 July. New from Brighton in 1946, No 34021 was a much-travelled loco through the years, serving the extremes of the SR system at Plymouth and London and many other places in between.

1968
THE END
OF STEAM
2008

SPL 9
34021

PLATFORM BARROWS

Opposite left **London (Waterloo):** Moments later and *Dartmoor* backs out of the gloom – of light and mood – of Waterloo and, overseen by Big Ben beyond, prepares to pass the famed Waterloo signalbox and travel the short distance to Nine Elms shed and oblivion. Just two enthusiasts adorn the platform end to snap 'just one last picture'!

Right: Platform Barrows Back in the 1950s and 1960s the number of people employed at each station was generally far higher than it is today. The Railway Porter was a

feature of all but the smallest of stations. They were to many passengers the 'salt of the earth' stepping forward with a smile and a caring hand to assist as an elderly or less mobile passenger stepped down from the train. He would often as not have a platform barrow to hand on which to stack the passenger's heavy luggage. He would then escort the passenger to the station exit where he would, if required, hail the next available cab. The cost for all this care and attention? Well amazingly it was all at the passenger's discretion! Platform barrows today... where are they when you need them? Are there still Porters? *PT*

Below **Nine Elms:** On view on 7 May was 'Merchant Navy' Class 4-6-2 No 35023 *Holland-Afrika Line*, 'Standard' Class 5 4-6-0 No 73022 and 'Standard' Class 4 2-6-4T No 80012. The 'Merchant Navy' Pacific was new in January 1949 and served a number of sheds between stints at Exmouth Junction and, finally, Nine Elms. No 73022 by comparison, was two years younger, emerging in November 1951, initially as a BR(MR) engine at Chester shed. A move two years later to WR duties saw it at Swindon by 1954, when it was transferred to the SR, by way of Weymouth. When seen here, it was a Nine Elms resident but already out of use and withdrawn officially a week after this view. No 80012 was also new in 1951, but was a Southern loco throughout its life. Mostly operating on the ex-LB&SCR route, it ended up at Eastleigh and was withdrawn on 15 March 1967, two months before this view and one wonders how it ended up here. A second 'Merchant Navy' Class 4-6-2 No 35007 *Aberdeen Commonwealth,* complete with front number plate, but, sadly, without name, looks in fine condition as it stands alongside the 'Old Shed'. Though they were around until the very end, they and the nominally 'junior' 'WC/BBs' worked cheek-by-jowl and with the latter having greater numbers, the 'MNs' tended to be seen less often. A long time servant of Salisbury shed, a move to Weymouth in January 1965 was followed by decampment to Nine Elms a month before this view, on 17 April. It survived until the very end in July but, sadly, was not to be one of the lucky ones saved for preservation *MJS*

Right **On shed:** Now the home of the 'new' Covent Garden fruit and vegetable market, Nine Elms was once the proud home of one of the Southern Railway's most prestigious depots, preparing and maintaining many of the crack express locomotives. The London & Southampton Railway provided the first facility in the area in 1838, on the opposite side of the line to the final destination and closer to Waterloo. This was replaced by two buildings in different locations around Nine Elms Goods Yard, before the final pitch close to Crimsworth Road opened in 1876. Thereafter, two large constructions – known respectively as 'Old Shed' and 'New Shed' – took over the main housing for locos in 1885 and 1910. In the far southern corner was a turntable for locos' use and in later years a substantial block of flats, which gave a wondrous view of the shed yard, overlooked this.

On 7 May 1967, 'Battle of Britain' Class 4-6-2 No 34090 *Sir Eustace Missenden Southern Railway* – once more devoid of its proud name – has turned and makes its way slowly back towards the shed. Drivers and crew were always very conscious of good neighbourliness and respected the needs of the flats dwellers. The loco had been named at Waterloo on 15 February 1949, when new, by the man himself; and it had been rebuilt from Bullied's original design in August 1960. *MJS*

The last two at Nine Elms shed

Above **Nine Elms:** A view very rarely noticed by travellers and even more rarely photographed. Captured from a passing train, we see the back of Nine Elms shed on 7 August 1967 and witness that a month after the end of steam on the SR, there is still steam at the depot, albeit not in use. 'West Country' Class 4-6-2 Nos 34047 *Callington* and No 34034 *Honiton*, separated by four empty wagons, stand forlornly among the remnants of the once-great shed, awaiting their call for their very last journey. New in the tag end of 1946, No 34047 began life at Exmouth Junction, thence moving to Salisbury and Brighton in quick succession in the summer of 1951. Nine Elms was host for eight months to June 1959, before the final trip to Bournemouth. By comparison, *Honiton* was a few months older and began its BR life at Stewarts Lane. Service at Plymouth (Friary), Exmouth Junction and Eastleigh followed before a final residency at Nine Elms. Both survived to the very end of steam on the SR but neither managed to achieve preservation.

A Selection of 1967 Station Closures (all Regions)

2 January	Elswick,	Gilsland,	Wetheral,	Chorlton-cum-Hardy,
	Stockport	Tiviot Dale,	Cheadle Heath,	Featherstone,	Pontefract
	Tanshelf,	Forest Row,	Withyam,	Needham,	Haughley,
	Six Mile Bottom,		Fulbourne,	Rowfant	Long Eaton
30 January	Bodmin General		Bodmin North,	Dunmere Halt,	Wadebridge,
	Padstow				
6 March	Ferryhill (Durham),		Ripon,	Batley,	Ravensthorpe,
	Buxton (ex-Midland),		Monkwearmouth,		Budleigh Salterton,
	Sidmouth,	Ottery St Mary,	Sidmouth Junction,		Linton,
	Haverhill,	Sturmer,	Long Melford,	Somersham,	Chatteris,
	Chapel-en-le-Frith,		Peak Forest,	Millers Dale,	Bakewell,
	Rowsley,	Matlock Bath,	Derby Nottingham Road,		Lydd Town,
	New Romney & Littlestone-on-Sea				
29 April	Leeds Central				
1 May	Stanningley				
5 June	South Aylesbury Halt				
4 September	Laurencekirk,	Coupar	Angus,	Forfar,	Bridge of Dun,
	Nottingham Victoria,		Easthaven,	West Ferry	

REFRESHMENTS

Above **Basingstoke shed:** officially closed in March 1963, but such was its strategic geogeraphical position, that it stayed in place as a servicing point for steam locos right to the end of steam on the SR. Thus, on 2 July 1967, a wonderfully clean 'Standard' Class 5 4-6-0 No 73029 stands with a classmate, enjoying the afternoon rays of the summer sunshine. It began life on 26 January 1952, a long way away, at Blackpool (Central) shed! October 1953 saw it move south to Bristol (St Philips Marsh) but swiftly on, two months later to Carmarthen, in deepest West Wales. That was for just one month, after which Bristol again beckoned, before Swindon, Weymouth, Eastleigh, Guildford and, finally, in October 1966, Nine Elms. *MJS*

Below **Basingstoke shed:** At the side of the 1905-vintage shed on the same day, stood 'Standard' Class 5 4-6-0 No 73018 and 'Standard' Class 4 2-6-4T No 80152. New in November 1951 and 1956 respectively, the 'Standard 5' began as BR(MR) loco at Nottingham, before progressively migrating to the WR and then SR, arriving at Weymouth in 1958. No 80152 was first around Brighton before gravitating west and ending up at Eastleigh in October 1966. The shed buildings seen here were the third provided to serve Basingstoke, all on different sites. The L&SWR built the first in 1839, south of the line west of the station; the Berks & Hants Railway built the second, in 1850, north and east and this lasted 100 years! The third of the trio, in 1905, replaced the L&SWR facility and was on the opposite side of the tracks to this when the station was enlarged. *MJS*

Name	Class	Number	To Island	Disposal
Cowes (cont)	Brighton 0-6-0	IWC10	1900	To mainland 1936
	Adams '02' 0-4-4	W15	1936	Scrapped 1956
Fishbourne	Stroudley 'Alx' 0-6-0	W9	1930	To mainland 1936
	Adams '02' 0-4-4	W14	1936	Scrapped 1967
Freshwater	Stephenson 0-6-0	Not numbered	1886	Contractor's loco. To mainland c1890
	Stroudley 'A1' 0-6-0	FYN2, W2 Then W8	1913	To mainland 1949 then to IWSR 1979
	Adams '02' 0-4-4	W35	1949	Scrapped 1967
Godshill	Adams '02' 0-4-4	W25	1925	Scrapped 1963
Medina	Manning Wardie 0-6-0	FYN1	1913	Scrapped 1932
	Stroudley 'E1' 0-6-0	W1	1932	Scrapped 1957
Merstone	Adams '02' 0-4-4	W27	1926	Scrapped 1967
Mill Hill	Black Hawthorn 0-4-2	IWC3	1870	To mainland 1918
Newport	Hawthorn 2-2-2	IWC6	1875	Scrapped 1895
	Stroudley 'A1' 0-6-0	IWC11	1902	To mainland 1947 then to IWSR 1974
	Adams '02' 0-4-4	W34	1947	Scrapped 1955
Ningwood	Adams '02' 0-4-4	W18	1930	Scrapped 1966
Osborne	Beyer Peacock 2-4-0	IWC5	1876	Scrapped 1926
	Adams '02' 0-4-4	W19	1923	Scrapped 1955
Ryde	Beyer Peacock 2-4-0	Not numbered W13	1864	Scrapped 1940
	Stroudley 'E1' 0-6-0	W3	1932	Scrapped 1959
Sandown	Beyer Peacock 2-4-0	Not numbered	1864	Scrapped 1923
	Adams '02' 0-4-4	W21	1924	Scrapped 1966
Seaview	Adams '02' 0-4-4	W17	1930	Scrapped 1967
Shanklin	Beyer Peacock 2-4-0	Not numbered W14	1864	Scrapped 1927
	Adams '02' 0-4-4	W20	1923	Scrapped 1967
Shorwell	Adams '02' 0-4-4	W30	1926	Scrapped 1965
St. Helens	Unknown class 2-4-0	Not numbered	c1881 or 1863	Scrapped 1927 Scrapped 1967 Scrapped 1965 Contractor's loco. Sold in 1893 to contractor for the Newport, Godshill & St. Lawrence Railway. Renamed *St. Lawrence*. (See also *Brading*)
St. Lawrence	Unknown class 2-4-0	Not numbered	c1881 or 1863	See above Scrapped 1898
Totland	Adams '02' 0-4-4	W23	1925	Scrapped 1955
Whippingham	Beyer Peacock 4-4-0	IWC7	1906	Scrapped 1926
Whitwell	Adams '02' 0-4-4	W26	1925	Scrapped 1966
Wroxall	Beyer Peacock 2-4-0	Not numbered W16	1872	Scrapped 1933
	Stroudley 'E1' 0-6-0	W4	1933	Scrapped 1960
Ventnor	Beyer Peacock 2-4-0	Not numbered W15	1868	Scrapped 1925
	Stroudley 'A1' 0-6-0	IWC12	1903	To mainland 1936
	Adams '02' 0-4-4	W16	1936	Scrapped 1967
Yarmouth	Stroudley 'E1' 0-6-0	W2	1932	Scrapped 1956

List of Isle of Wight locomotives carrying Island place names
Continued from Page 65

W20 at Ryde

W28 at Ventnor

Ryde Locoshed

W35 at Ryde

to Norwood Junction on 30 July 1962 and then, for the rest of the decade, to Feltham on 17 December of that year. TOPS gave it a new persona of No 08203 in March 1974 and it quietly plied its trade until 'fame' was determined when it was chosen as one of three of the class to have their cabs cut-down in height, to accommodate freight traffic over a restricted branch from Pantyffynnon. Renumbered 08991 in January 1986, it was named *Kidwelly* on 18th at Llanelli but, sadly, traffic was not to be as expected and the loco was withdrawn from Landore shed on 23 June 1987. *MJS*

Left **Guildford:** We have seen plenty of 'big engines', valiantly at work on what they did best even up to the end, but the smaller locomotives also gave sterling service. Among these were the strangely designed (to UK eyes) 'USA Tanks'. Initially introduced in 1942 to a U.S. Army Transportation Corps design, the Southern Railway bought a number in 1946, modifying them where necessary to suit the UK market. In the last days, some were still plying their trade and, on 7 July 1967, 'USA' Class 0-6-0T No 30072 stands ever hopeful at the entrance to Guildford's 'half-roundhouse'. Allocated to and working in and around Southampton Docks for most of its UK existence, it eventually had a transfer to Guildford on 4 March 1963 and, thus, by the time of its eventual withdrawal on 9 July had only served two depots.

minimum of attention that could keep them running. 'Merchant Navy' Class 4-6-2 No 35023 *Holland-Afrika Line* – seen lurking on *page 89* – is now out in the open moments later, dragged and pushed there by '08' diesel shunter D3273. As already noted, it was withdrawn in March from Eastleigh and perhaps the shunter is positioning it for its final trip to the knacker's yard. Just a humble shunter at this time, D3273 was to go on to have a far more interesting career than its more illustrious neighbour here. New on 11 October 1956, as No 13273, it was despatched to Hither Green shed, where it stayed until a move

Top **Basingstoke:** On 23 July Bo-B0 Type 3 D6542 hauls loco 'Standard' Class 4 2-6-4T No 80151, 'Standard' Class 4 2-6-0 No 76058 & 'Standard' Class 4 2-6-4T No 80148 through Basingstoke on what was thought to be their last journey. However No 80151 turned out to be one of the lucky ones having been purchased from Dai Woodham's yard in Barry in 1974 by a group from Essex, but moved to The Bluebell Railway in 1998 where she returned to service in 2001.

Right: Despite the disparity in size of classes – 110 'WC/BBs' as opposed to a mere 30 'MNs' – we have been rather disparaging in representing the latter, so here is another view of the tired locomotives that were pressed into service with the

Above **Birmingham (Snow Hill):** This may seem a strange place to start for a look at the Cambrian, but Birmingham (Snow Hill) station was the 'portal' through which many thousands travelled on their way into Wales and to the Cambrian Coast. Our photographer is appropriately aboard the *Cambrian Coast Express* of 9 July 1966 as it leaves the station, passing station pilot '5700' Class 0-6-0PT No 8767 and, right, a diesel shunter resting between duties. No 8767 had survived up to and beyond the end of steam on BR(WR) at Oxley (Wolverhampton) shed and by the time of this view was an incumbent of Stourbridge Junction shed, which, by now, was under MR jurisdiction. It only lasted another month, however, being dispensed with at Croes Newydd on 13 August 1966.

...We lost

1967

Steam on The Cambrian Coast

1968
THE END
OF STEAM
2008

The *Cambrian Coast Express* like its counterpart *The Pines Express* on the Somerset & Dorset will be long remembered as the starting point for many a family holiday. Starting its journey at London Paddington and travelling via Bicester, Banbury, Leamington Spa, Birmingham (Snow Hill), Wolverhampton (Low Level), the *Express* would arrive at Shrewsbury normally behind a Castle Class 4-6-0. Shrewsbury was where, for most railway enthusiasts in the post war years, the interest level would rise dramatically.

Why? Well a real treat could be in store!

This is where the locomotive would be changed but not normally for any of the more common types. Until the late 1950s the chances were high of the *Express* being hauled out of Shrewsbury by a pair of the famous 'Dukedog' 4-4-0 locomotives built at Swindon Works between 1930 and 1936, but the roots of which lay in the 1890s. To explain - the 'Dukedogs' were constructed from the frames of withdrawn examples of the 1902 built 'Bulldog' Class 4-4-0 combined with the cabs and other parts from the 1890s built 'Duke'

Class 4-4-0s. The boilers were however newly built, thereby classifying them as 'new' locomotives. The GWR recognised that in spite of considerable advances in locomotive design in the years 1902-1936 the need for a lightweight tender locomotive for branch and secondary line work was ever present and rather than re-invent the wheel the economic sense of reusing parts of withdrawn locomotives, and constructing to a proven wheel arrangement made for a sound policy.

The alternative to the double headed 'Dukedog' was an almost equally interesting 'Manor' Class 4-6-0 which progressively replaced the 'Dukedogs' and were, together with the 'Standard' Class 4, 4-6-0s & 2-6-0s the mainstay of the Cambrian line from Shrewsbury to Aberystwyth during the latter days of steam. The last of the 'Manors' were withdrawn in December 1965 leaving the final workings in the hands of the Class 4s.

Meanwhile back on the Cambrian Coast Express

Left **Shrewsbury:** Many miles further west, Shrewsbury was the main gateway to things Cambrian from England, being only a relatively few miles from Oswestry and access to the Cambrian Railways. We are still aboard the *Cambrian Coast Express* of 9 July and the engine shed is glimpsed as the train leaves Shrewsbury station and makes its way west. Closest to the main line is the ex-LMS side of the shed complex and here we see 'Standard' Class 4 4-6-0 No 75016, 'Standard' 'Black 5' 4-6-0 No 45311 and 'Standard' Class 2 2-6-0 No 78018 as well as another couple of Stanier locos. Behind them is the 10-road facility of 1877, initially provided by the L&NWR and, to the left, the ex-GWR 1883 structures.

Welshpool: Venturing yet further into Wales, we pause at Welshpool on 9 July. Our journey from Birmingham has been handled by 'Standard' Class 4 2-6-0 No 76038, left and it is now to be partnered forward by 'Standard' Class 4 4-6-0 No 75013, which waits alongside to come forward as pilot. The rather crudely painted 'shedplate' on the smokebox of No 76038, would seem to indicate it is under the control of Saltley (Birmingham) shed —an ex-LMS shed handling expresses on the ex-Cambrian/GWR? It had moved there in August 1964, having previously been on ex-LNER and LMS metals, allocated to New England (Peterborough) and Cricklewood. Its sojourn at Saltley lasted until 18 June 1966, when it was transferred to Machynlleth and, thus, it is working on home territory in this view but its new 'owners' have not seen fit to expunge the '2E' legend. No 75013 is also devoid of shedplate (and front numberplate) — such was the state of affairs in these latter days. Into the 21st century and the locos would be standing on tarmac, as Welshpool has been 'graced' with a far more Spartan, island platform, to the right of this view, with a main road now taking the erstwhile trackbed. Thankfully, the magnificent station building, left, is still extant but now only operating as a retail outlet.

having left Shrewsbury the line heads towards the Welsh Border passing through Buttington Junction (*station closed 1960*) where the Cambrian Railway's erstwhile route from Oswestry to Newtown ran in until that route's final closure between Oswestry and Buttington in 1965.

On arrival at Welshpool, the next station on the route, the narrow gauge Welshpool & Llanfair Light Railway could be seen running in to the far side boundary of the goods yard until final closure to goods traffic in 1963. Thankfully the majority of this delightful narrow gauge line was saved by a dedicated group of enthusiasts and reopened in stages from Castle Caerinion back to a new station at

Welshpool (Raven Square) opened in 1982. Sadly it did not prove possible to save the relatively short section running through the backs of the town houses and across the road to the main line station.

Leaving Welshpool the standard gauge line heads south to Forden (*station closed 14 June 1965*) where research shows that back on 3 December 1891 two young lads conspired to steal the sum of thirteen shillings from the ticket office cash box. Just four days later they had not only been caught but were sentenced at Montgomery Petty Sessions - the punishment being 12 strokes of the birch administered by a police constable!* How times have changed! Montgomery

* (More details at the time of writing can be found at the fascinating web site *Powys A day in the life* the link address is *http://a-day-in-the-life.powys.org.uk/eng/law/el_juve1.php*)

Above **Welshpool** A few minutes on from the last page and we are now underneath the B4381 road bridge in Welshpool and witnessing 'Standard' Class 4 4-6-0 No 75013 having coupled up to 'Standard' Class 4 2-6-0 No 76038 and ready to depart with the ongoing *Cambrian Coast Express* of 9 July. The long platform of the station, left, is still present in 2008, but with the tarmac now replacing rails. Compared to its companion, which was withdrawn from Machynlleth in September

1966, No 75013 survived its term in mid-Wales to end its days at Stoke exactly a year later. New on 1 December 1951, No 75013 was the older of the two seen here by nearly three years and had something of a nomadic existence, serving first Patricroft and then Llandudno Junction, Chester, Mold Junction, Bletchley, Machynlleth, Shrewsbury, Croes Newydd and, finally, Stoke.

Below **Machynlleth:** shed has always been a fascinating place.

Somewhat cramped against a rock wall, and tucked away in mid-Wales, away from the hurly burly of much of the UK's railway system, it nevertheless had a wide variety of interesting and often ancient locomotives allocated to it over the years. On the extreme western edge of Montgomeryshire, the first facility, a three-road straight shed, was built by the Newtown & Machynlleth Railway in 1863 and extended to the north by a two-road addition by the Cambrian

some time later. Closed to steam from 5 December 1966, it was turned over to servicing DMUs – and the occasional visiting diesel loco. The elder of the two sheds is seen with more modern motive power present on 9 July 1966, as 'Standard' Class 4 4-6-0 No 75048 stands waiting for the next call. This shed was demolished by 1996, but, more recently the whole complex has been revitalised by large expenditure in fitting the depot for 21st century duties.

MEN EMPLOYED BY FARMERS MUST NOT CROSS THE MAIN LINES TO FETCH MILK CANS

Right **Welshpool:** *Cambrian Coast Express* departing with a flourish behind 'Manor' Class 4-6-0 No 7823 *Hook Norton Manor* in April 1962 with headboard.

Below **Machynlleth** We are now back with *Cambrian Coast Express* of 9 July, seen from a vantage point immediately to the west of the station, as the locos pause for intake of water from the adjacent tower. The ten-coach express is strung out behind the two engines and the length of the train helps to show off the change of gradients through the station. The train would split here, with portions going to Aberystwyth and Pwllheli and, moments later, there would be even more shunting than normal, as these two locos were despatched to nearby Dovey Junction to retrieve a failed DMU, which was blocking the path to Barmouth and beyond. 'Standard' Class 4 4-6-0 No 75004 was then brought from the sidings at Machynlleth to take forward the Aberystwyth part of the *CCE*.

would, until closure in 14 June 1965, have been the next available station at which to alight; although it was some two miles from the town. It still seems remarkable that this one time county town of the erstwhile county of Montgomeryshire no longer boasts a railway station, in spite of the fact that the line still passes this way. As the train approaches Abermule it passes the site of the tragic accident that occurred on 26 January 1921 when a west bound stopping train, from Whitchurch, crashed head-on with an east bound express from Aberystwyth. Seventeen people were killed including the driver and fireman of the stopping train and a director of The Cambrian Railway one Lord Herbert Vane-Tempest. The cause of the accident was found to be the ability, at the time, for conflicting movements to be possible at Abermule. A number of changes resulted following the enquiry including the tablet machine being moved to the signal box and placed under the strict control of the signalman.

Abermule was the junction for a short branch to Kerry, passenger services ended on the branch in 1931 but goods trains ran until final closure on 1 May 1956. There was also an extensive (c 3 miles) 2' gauge tramway system, linking to the branch at the Kerry end, which predominantly transported timber - but this was all gone before the 1930s. Abermule station closed its doors for

Below **Dovey Junction:** As mentioned on the previous page, 'Standard' Class 4 4-6-0 No 75004 was summoned to depart with the Aberystwyth portion of the CCE, whilst the two 'Standards' already seen were despatched to rescue the failed DMU at Dovey Junction. This is the view shortly before the departure, with footplate crew discussing re-arrangements with the station staff. Having begun the long journey from Paddington at 11.10 a.m., the time would now be around 4.30 p.m. and there would normally be a maximum of five minutes between arrival at Machynlleth and departure of the Aberystwyth section. Some passengers wander around the platform, no doubt somewhat bemused and/or confused as to what is to happen, especially if they had been originally seated in the wrong portion! No 75004 was another well-travelled loco, emerging as new on 31 August 1951 and surviving until withdrawal, from Shrewsbury shed, on 25 March 1967.

Main picture **Barmouth:** Without doubt, the major and most impressive structure on the line from Machynlleth to Pwllheli was the Barmouth Bridge, taking both rails and a foot toll bridge across the Mawddach Estuary. With the water near low tide and looking

across the estuary towards the beach around Fairbourne, 'Standard' Class 4 4-6-0 No 75055 heads towards Barmouth as it crosses the bridge with the once daily down freight, consisting of 27 mainly box wagons plus guard's brakevan and including a gunpowder wagon for the Works at Penrhyndeudraeth. In the 21st century, goods traffic over the Cambrian route is virtually non-existent, having been in decline over the previous four decades. The gunpowder Works at Penrhyn closed during the 1990s and the oil trains to Aberystwyth also ceased during the same decade, but even here, on 11 July 1966, there is but one non-passenger service a day! No 75055 was delivered new as late as 26 January 1957, initially to Bedford. Frequent moves to other sheds on the MML, including

to Leicester twice (January 1960-February 1961 and February –September 1962), came before a switch to the WCML and a move to Bletchley on 25 May 1963. Shrewsbury, Machynlleth and Croes Newydd were then homes before a final move back to England, to Stoke and eventual withdrawal on 15 July 1967.

The 900-yds bridge was built by the Aberystwyth and Welsh Coast Railway and opened in 1867. As built, it included a lifting drawbridge section to permit the passage of tall ships and was constructed entirely of wood. The drawbridge section, at the northern end of the bridge, was rebuilt in 1901 as a swing bridge with two steel spans. This facility is still available (glimpsed on the right of this view) but rarely used.

Serious doubts surfaced in 1980 concerning the safety of the ageing wooden structure, as a type of marine worm was attacking it and there were concerns that the line would be closed because of it but, happily, investment was found and the structure properly repaired. However, the weight of modern locomotives then led to an initial ban on locomotive-hauled trains, which brought the immediate cessation of the diminishing freight traffic north of Tywyn, including explosives traffic to and from the factory at Penrhyndeudraeth, as already noted. That traffic was re-routed via Maentwrog Road railway station and the Conwy Valley Line, before closure of the Works.

the last time on 14 June 1965 and now trains simply pass by on their way to Newtown. Thankfully the station at Newtown is very much open for business in 2008, although the first station here on The Llanidloes and Newtown Railway, the first railway to reach the town in 1859, closed just two years after the opening! The reason being that in 1861 The Newtown and Machynlleth Railway entered the town and their new station served both companies which together with The Oswestry, Ellesmere and Whitchurch Railway, Oswestry and Newtown Railway, merged to become The Cambrian Railway in July 1864.

Passing through the small hamlet of Scafell where there was 'twice' a halt the first 1863-1891 and the second 1913 - 1955 the once busy junction at Moat Lane is reached where even in 1967 trains would no longer stop - the station having closed five years previously. This was where the line to Llanidloes and Three Cocks Junction joined, it was closed to all traffic on 2 October 1967. Caersws the next station has fared somewhat better and those with an interest in romantic poetry may be interested to know that John Ceiriog Hughes the respected Welsh poet and lyricist was Station Master here from 1868 until his parting of this life in 1877. This station was also the starting point for trains to Garth & Van Road and the Quarry beyond. In order to have travelled on this byway you would have had to have been here before 1940. Constructed to carry the ore from the lead mines at Van and Dylife, it was like many of the

1968
THE END
OF STEAM
YEARS
2008

Below **Barmouth:** We have already seen 'Standard' Class 4 4-6-0 No 75013 on *Cambrian Coast Express* duty on 9 July and we now have another glimpse of it two days later, on the same turn. Threading through the narrow access route permitted to the railway, the late afternoon sunshine of around 5.45 p.m. casts shadows from the retaining wall but nicely highlights the locomotive as it approaches Barmouth station. It is sad that, at this date, the former imperative of hosting the magnificent headboard on the locomotive's smokebox, announcing the train, has been dispensed with!

Known in Welsh as Abermaw (formally) or Y Bermo (colloquially), Barmouth town grew around a shipbuilding industry and then, more recently, as a seaside resort. Notable among the buildings in the town are the mediaeval tower house and the 19th century Ty Crwn roundhouse prison, whereas a newer attraction is a new Lifeboat Visitors' Centre, where visitors can purchase souvenirs and take a look at the lifeboat from the viewing gallery. The busy harbour plays host to the annual Three Peaks yacht race. William Wordsworth, a visitor to Barmouth in the 19th century, described it as being… "With a fine sea view in front, the mountains behind, the glorious estuary running eight miles inland and Cadair Idris within compass of a day's walk, Barmouth can always hold its own against any rival." Geographically it is the closest seaside resort to the West Midlands and, consequently, a large proportion of its tourist visitors, as well as its permanent residents, are from Wolverhampton, Birmingham, Dudley and other parts of the Black Country.

original lines of the Cambrian Railways in the area, created by the industrialist and entrepreneur, David Davies. Davies will best be remembered for establishing his own railway from Rhondda, where coal was extracted, to his own dock at Barry for export. His house at Llandinam, Broneirion, overlooks the village and is at the time of writing the Welsh Girl Guide Training Centre. As our journey so far shows 14 June 1965 was a black day for the route of the *Cambrian Coast Express* and the next six stations Pontdolgoch, Carno, Tallerdig, Llanbrynmair, Commins Coch Halt and Cemmes Road all closed to passengers on the same day. Cemmes Road was until 1950 a junction with a line going northwards to Dinas Mawddwy, with intermediate stations at Cemmaes, Aberangell and Mallwyd, passenger services on this branch ended as early as 1 January 1931 and the line closed to all traffic on 1 July 1951.

On arrival at Machynlleth the *Cambrian Coast Express* would split into two portions:
• The first travelling to Aberystwyth via Dovey Junction, Glandyfi *(Closed 14 June 1965)*, Ynyslas *(Closed 14 June 1965)*, Borth, Llandre *(Closed 14 June 1965)* and Bow Street *(Closed 14 June 1965)*.

• The second portion would go forward to Pwllheli via Dovey Junction, Gogarth Halt *(Closed 14 June 1965)*, Abertafol Halt *(Last train called on 14 May 1984 but closed officially on 30 September 1985)*, Penhelig Halt, Aberdovey, Tywyn, Tonfanau, Llangelynin Halt *(Closed 25 October 1991)*, Fairbourne, Dollgellau, Penmaenpool, Arthog, Morfa Mawddach, Barmouth, Llanaber, Talybont, Ardudwy, Duffryn, Llanbedr, Pensarn, Llandanwg,

Below **Dovey Junction:** This station is virtually unattainable by foot and there is no road access. Thus, in normal times it is a very quiet and sometimes desolate spot, but, especially in steam days, it came alive at odd periods when more than one train arrived at the same time. Such is the view here, on 12 July 1966, when this day's *CCE* is seen arriving behind 'Standard' Class 4 4-6-0 No 75016. In this morning shot, the Aberystwyth portion behind the 'Standard' was due to reach here around 10.20 a.m. and then await the ex-Pwllheli set some few minutes later. However, on Saturdays, several of the intermediate stops were excluded on the longer run, with coaches from the northern outpost arriving at 10.17 a.m., ahead of the Aberystwyth train. With those standing to the right here, the Aberystwyth set must have been running a little late. No 75016 will then move out of the station and back onto the waiting stock from Pwllheli, before taking the whole train forward to Machynlleth and then on to Wolverhampton and Paddington. Final arrival in the metropolis would be at 4 p.m., or 4.06 p.m. on Saturdays. To the left, a Shrewsbury-Aberystwyth DMU service awaits the road for the thirty minute trip to reach the coast. No 75016 began its career at Southport on 26 January 1952, before moving to respectively Nuneaton, Shrewsbury and Croes Newydd. It ended its days as a stationary boiler at Colwick (Nottingham) from 24 June to 15 July 1967!

Below **Newtown:** Having shared some of the sights and experiences of our photographer during his brief holiday in mid-Wales and his view of the *Cambrian Coast Express* on various days, we are now with him on his journey back towards England. Again aboard the CCE, we are treated to a brief view of Newtown, as we head for Welshpool. Class 2 2-6-0 No 46521 waits to head in the opposite direction with a very short special of cement wagons. The hilly terrain around the railway here can be judged by the escarpment that is the garden of the house on the hillside. 46521 was another loco built in British Railways days to an earlier design, this time from H A Ivatt in 1946. For some reason known as a 'Mickey Mouse', members of this Class were well liked by crews and they served all around the UK, in all regions by their final demise. This particular example was new from Swindon Works on 21 February 1953 and was a BR(WR) loco throughout its life. Its first allocation was to Oswestry but for only a month before a rapid shift to Brecon, for duties on trains radiating from that centre. Oswestry had the engine back again from 31 October 1959, before a final move to Machynlleth came on 9 March 1963. The end came there on 30 October 1966, but happily that was not the end, as preservation beckoned, initially

on the Severn Valley Railway, where it achieved some fame in the BBC TV *'Oh! Dr Beeching'* series. It also acquired the name Blossom through this series! At the time of writing, it was undergoing overhaul on the Great Central Railway.

Main picture **Morfa Mawddach:** On the following day, we are back in the Barmouth area, but this time on the opposite side of the estuary to the town itself. Once more enjoying his ride on the day's *CCE* we are arriving at Morfa Mawddach station, the junction for the Cambrian branch to Dolgellau, where it would form an end-on junction with the GWR from Bala. 'Greek meets Greek' here, as 'Standard' Class 4 4-6-0 No 75013, yet again on the express, passes 'Standard' Class 4 4-6-0 No 75055 with the one down freight of the day, with yet another 'ragged' mix of wagons.

Though the branch to Dolgellau has long since gone, the station is still popular with people wishing to visit Barmouth, as the trip across by train is far shorter than long road journey around the estuary. Formerly known as Barmouth Junction, the services to Dolgellau and beyond were withdrawn in 1965. Originally a four-platform station, it is now a single platform unstaffed halt. Trains stop on request. The former branch trackbed is now a popular walk alongside the estuary.

Harlech, Tygwyn, Talsarnau, Llandecwyn, Penrhyndeudraeth, Minffordd, Porthmadog, Black Rock Halt *(Closed August 1976)*, Criccieth, Afonwen, Penychain Halt and Aberech.

Of all the stations along the route perhaps Penychain Halt is amongst the most well known as this is the station that served the Butlins Pwllheli Holiday Camp, indeed in 1993 the station was renamed Butlin's Penychain. The camp is now owned by Haven Holidays and is known as Hafan Y Môr Holiday Park the station has now reverted to Penychain and at the time of writing is a request stop.

Below **Welshpool:** Our final view of the ex-Cambrian Railway metals again portrays the express that bore the magical name, *Cambrian Coast Express* – again sadly without headboard. On 12 July 1966, 'Standard' Class 4 4-6-0 No 75012 slows for the Welshpool stop on the approach from Shrewsbury. The time is just after 3 p.m. and the weather has closed in. Yet another of the 'Standard 4' 4-6-0s that monopolised the working in these later days, No 75012 was new on 1 December 1951, to Patricroft in Manchester. There were various moves thereafter, from 3 October 1953, mostly in and around the North Wales Coast and slightly further inland, before a final home came at Shrewsbury on 19 March 1966. It is therefore working from this shed when seen here and had literally only just been returned to steam in this week, following a brief term out of use. Withdrawal was on 28 Janaury 1967, a little over 15 years old!

1968
THE END
OF STEAM
40 YEARS
2008

North Blyth: The next in line to see the end, blanking out yet another swathe of the UK to steam operation, was the North East of England. The birthplace of our railways over 140 years earlier, it was perhaps fitting that this area should have fought the marauding enemy to within 12 months of final capitulation. On the northern fringes of the area, some 13 miles north of Newcastle, were North and South Blyth sheds, separated by the River Blyth as it approached the North Sea. A journey between the two was by ferry. Dating from the 12th century, the port has changed dramatically over recent years, with the erstwhile mainstays of the main industries that helped the town prosper shipbuilding, with the salt trade, fishing and the railways also playing an important role – drastically reducing or disappearing altogether. The port still thrives, however, with the shipping of paper and pulp from Scandinavia for the newspaper industries of England and Scotland. To help transhipment, especially of coal, large staithes were built into the tidal river and an example, striking out from the northern bank, is seen in the late afternoon of 1 July 1967. The sheer size of the structure can be judged from the semaphore signals being dwarfed. *MJS*

At the birth of British Railways in 1948, the Eastern and North Eastern areas had been kept separate, with the sheds operating within the set boundaries allocated their own range of codes, despite the two being previously 'unified' within the LNER post-1923. As seen elsewhere, all this changed on 1 January 1967, when the two merged into one Eastern Region, with headquarters in York.

In 1948, the North Eastern Region had 32 'parent' sheds, with sub-sheds allocated to many of them. Over the next 19 years, there had been much swapping of territories, not least between the London Midland Region and both Eastern and North Eastern controls. Mostly this was to engulf the Sheffield and Leeds areas into ex-LNER province, but there was some lesser movement between ER and NER. Five of the sheds under ex-MR Leeds (Holbeck) jurisdiction moved to NER control (plus sub-shed Ilkley, which changed allegiance from Manningham to Leeds (Neville Hill)), as did the seven overseen by Wakefield; and three – Ardsley, Copley Hill and Bradford (Hammerton Street) left the ER to serve the NER. By the beginning of 1967, the

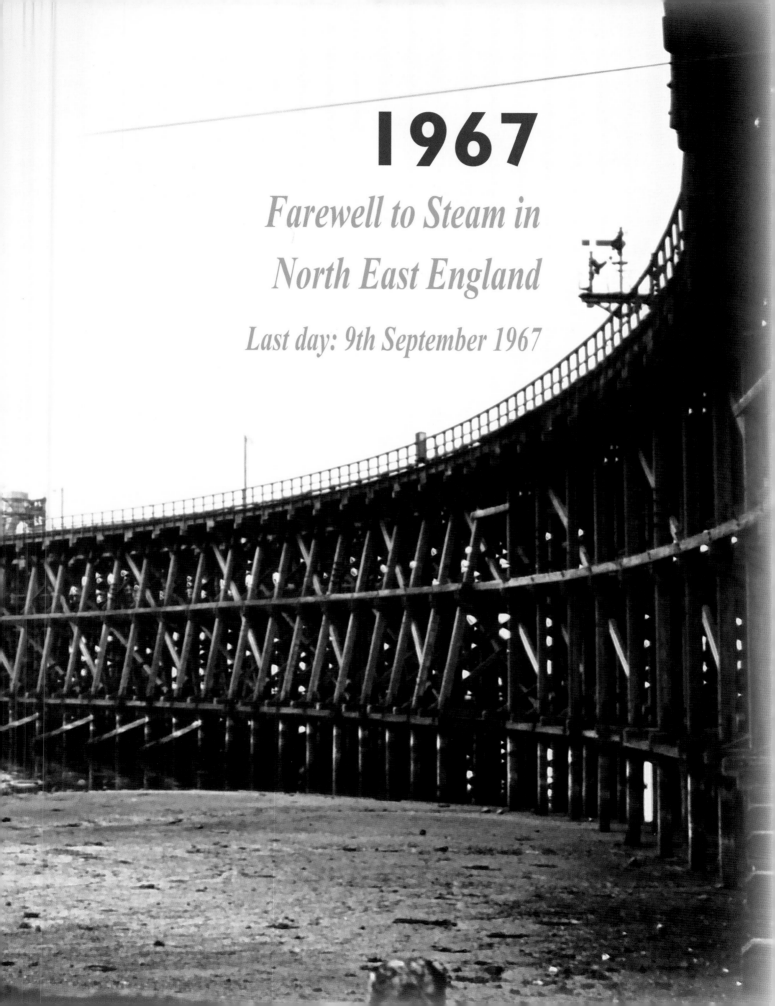

1967

Farewell to Steam in

North East England

Last day: 9th September 1967

Above **North Blyth:** Still on the north bank we are now inside North Blyth shed. Nominally with one code – 52F – the two Blyth sheds were 'separated' by the 'appendices' 'N' and 'S', with the latter being the first to close on 28 May 1967. North stayed open to the end and, on 1 July, Class '4' 2-6-0 Nos 43000 and No 43055 take shelter inside the roundhouse, although the summer weather was being kind on this day. Though designed by H A Ivatt in LMS days, the first of the class, No 43000, did not appear on the books until 21 February 1948, just two months into British Railways. Initially allocated to Crewe South, it moved around the system over the years, through Bletchley, Devon's Road (Bow), Nuneaton, Carlisle – Upperby, Canal and Kingmoor in quick succession – before transfer to BR(NER) on 27 August 1966. Blyth was its designated home and it stayed there until the very end on 9 September 1967. Its companion, No 43055, was younger by two years and was a NER loco for its entire life. Again a migratory bird, its final two allocations were to South Blyth in August 1966 and then moving across the river three months later. Its official end date was two weeks after this view, on 15 July 1967. *MJS*

number still open had shrunk considerably. Those remaining open for steam operation were:

Shed	Closure date	Closed to
York	25 June 1967	Steam
Hull (Dairycoates)	25 June 1967	Steam
Goole	25 June 1967	Steam
West Hartlepool	1 September 1967	Steam
North Blyth	1 September 1967	Steam
South Blyth	28 May 1967	Closed
Sunderland	1 September 1967	Closed
Tyne Dock	1 September 1967	Closed
Leeds (Holbeck)	1 December 1967	Steam
Stourton	15 January 1967	Steam
- ditto -	August 1967	Closed

Shed	Closure date	Closed to
Royston	4 November 1967	Steam
Normanton	30 September 1967	Steam
- ditto -	5 November 1967	Closed
Bradford (Manningham)	29 April 1967	Closed
Huddersfield	1 January 1967	Closed
Low Moor	30 September 1967	Closed
Wakefield	25 June 1967	Steam
Mirfield	2 January 1967	Steam

As with other regions of the UK's railway infrastructure, the North Eastern saw reduction in route mileage as well as locomotive operation – witness some of the stations and lines closed elsewhere in this section – but there were some positive developments. As the year opened, the first of four planned freightliner depots for the sector saw preliminary site work begin. Known as Tyne (Follingsby) Terminal, it was to serve both Tyneside and Wearside and was directly linked to the ECML. The other three to follow were at Stockton-on-Tees, Leeds (Stourton) and Hull. And the region was to benefit from the introduction of fast daytime inter-city services to King's Cross from 6 March. These included 13 trains each way from Newcastle, 12 from Darlington, 10 from Leeds, 9 each from York and Wakefield, 8 from Bradford and 2 from Harrogate. Also from 6 March, the two Pullman services between King's Cross and Sheffield were the only two direct services left to the city of steel; and the North Tyneside Electric service, opened in 1904 as one of the earliest in the country, switched to diesel operation, following its South Tyneside neighbour that had taken the same step four years earlier.

This was little comfort, however, to steam enthusiasts, who had seen the withdrawal in the closing months of 1966 of the specially air-pump-fitted '9Fs' that had given such sterling service on the Tyne Dock-Consett iron ore trains, not least up the 1-in-47 gradient from South Pelaw. Although the services survived, they were now operated by 'Type 2' diesels but, interestingly, the modern replacements were redirected via Gateshead, to avoid that climb! The last of the steam-hauled trains was on 19 November 1966, when '9F' Class 2-10-0 No 92063 was graced with 'The Tyne Docker' headboard. Elsewhere, rationalisation was also in the air at York. It was announced that the two 'halves' of York Railway Museum would be combined to integrate all exhibits into the Queen Street site, with the previous 'small exhibits' venue, housed in the old station buildings, closed, demolished and redeveloped.

13 April saw the fifth anniversary of the re-opening, by enthusiasts, of the Keighley & Worth Valley Railway and the line's centenary. Incorporated under an 1862 Act of Parliament, it was initially operated by the independent company, backed by the Midland Railway but, from 1881, the larger organisation took over control. Having enjoyed a brief period of prosperity, it suffered a decline post-WWI largely due to the onset of motor traffic, in common with many branch lines throughout the country. Diesel railcars had been introduced in 1960 to try and stem the losses, but without success and the branch close with the end of freight services in June 1962. By then, a number of enthusiasts had formed a society to save the line and the rest, as they say, is history. As is the story of another line 'born again' this year.

PORTERS

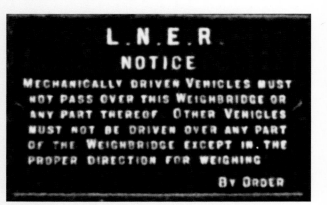

L.N.E.R.
NOTICE
MECHANICALLY DRIVEN VEHICLES MUST
NOT PASS OVER THIS WEIGHBRIDGE OR
ANY PART THEREOF. OTHER VEHICLES
MUST NOT BE DRIVEN OVER ANY PART
OF THE WEIGHBRIDGE EXCEPT IN. THE
PROPER DIRECTION FOR WEIGHING

BY ORDER

Appropriately north east of the K&WVR – and nearer the coast - the North Yorkshire Moors Railway (NYMR) Preservation Society was formed in 1967, initially focusing on securing the trackbed and (as a first step) only track from Grosmont through Goathland to Ellerbeck (about 6 miles). When the County Council and the National Park realised that a tourist railway ending in the middle of nowhere would be far less of an asset than one going all the way to Pickering, they arranged a rental-purchase arrangement with the NYMR to finance the additional twelve miles of track, with the results that can be seen today, with the line being among the top five of preserved lines in the UK.

Being the cradle of our railways and an area of large-scale mining, shipping and manufacturing, the northeast had many places of importance, not least among which was Kingston-upon-Hull. Nestling on the northern bank of the River Humber, the city was not to join the ever expanding railway map until 1840, after the Leeds & Selby Railway – incorporated by Act in 1830 – had decided against an extension to the port. It took the impetus from locals to secure a route into the area, but thereafter, things expanded substantially. The 'Railway Mania' of 1845 did not miss Hull and all manner of scheme were mooted. An early addition was an extension to the first line, to Bridlington – crossing no fewer than 37 roads on the level in the process. Paragon station was opened in 1848, giving the city a much more convenient entrance/ exit to the outside world. The succeeding years saw more proposals, from a variety of 'railways', resulting in a cat's cradle of lines into and around the city and no fewer than six locomotive shed sites over the years. At Nationalisation, four survived (one, Alexandra Dock, as a sub-shed) – Dairycoates (closed 21 September 1970), Botanic Gardens (6 May 1973)

the cutter's torch. Now preserved and named appropriately *Lord of The Isles,* she is owned by the North Eastern Locomotive Preservation Group, while spending some time on the North Yorkshire Moors Railway and other preserved lines, No 62005 *Lord of The Isles* is also a 'regular' on the main line, including use on *The Jacobite* summer season service from Fort William to Mallaig run by *West Coast Railway Company Ltd. MJS*

Left **Sunderland:** Whilst Blyth did see the incursion of ex-MR locos, Sunderland was to remain a stalwart NER shed until the end. Also seen on 1 July, this influence is highlighted by the presence of , *left to right,* ex-LNER 'J27' Class 0-6-0 Nos. 65817, 65789 and 65882. Initially Wilson Worsdell designed from 1906, later members, including No 65882 here, saw refinements by Vincent Raven from 1921. No 65817, without front numberplate here, was a long-term resident of Sunderland shed, leaving in February 1964 but returning thirteen months later, having been to Thornaby and Percy Main in the interim. Deletion from stock was on 27 May 1967. No 65789, a North Blyth incumbent for many years, transferred allegiance south of the river on 5 November 1966, before coming to Sunderland on 17 June 1967. The working stay was short, however, with the end decreed on 15 July. No 65882 was another wanderer as well as spending many years at Selby shed, before moving to Sunderland on 20 May 1967. This time, the end was to be the cessation of steam in the northeast on 9 September. The shed closed to steam officially on 17 September and the roundhouse, seen here, was demolished. The remaining buildings were then given over to diesels until the late-1980s and demolished in 1990. *MJS*

Right **Tyne Dock:** This shed was renowned for its specially adapted 9Fs, but it also housed many veteran NER locos and, at the close, a couple of preserved engines, including 'K1' Class 2-6-0 No 62005, seen here inside the shed on 1 July. It was another example of a loco built to basically an old design but appearing in the early years of Nationalisation. New on 31 August 1949, it was exactly a year before it received its first official shed allocation, to Heaton. Thereafter there were many moves before it ended up at Leeds

Holbeck in October 1967. It had been a Tyne Dock loco before this though without much work, as can be seen from this view, where an attempt has been made to rag the chimney! Withdrawn at the end of 1967, it was the last example of the class in service and, happily, thwarted

Main picture **West Hartlepool:**
Whether it is sheer age or
subsidence, the buildings at West
Hartlepool are in need of strong
support and obviously have been
for some time. On 1 July, a line of
five 'Austerities' fills the end road
through the shed, with work weary
'WD' Class 2-8-0 No 90459 poking
into the sunshine. Previously WD
8648 and LNER 3138, the ex-Ministry
of Supply locomotive became one
of a class of 733 examples inherited
by BR and was a stalwart of the
northeast throughout most of its
post-Nationalisation career, after a
brief spell at Colwick. Newport (in
the North Riding of Yorkshire) was
next, followed by Thornaby, Tyne
Dock and finally West Hartlepool. It
was withdrawn two weeks after this
view, but is presumably already out of
service, as it is missing its safety valve
cover. *MJS*

Left: Inside the shed, the shafts of sunlight attractively dappling the locos further exemplify the decrepitude of the structure. These include 'WD' Class 2-8-0 Nos. 90210, 90135 and 90434. The first and last were dispensed with on 15 July, whereas No 90135 survived until the end of steam in the region. *MJS*

Right: Just visible in the extreme left-hand portal of the left-hand view, the loco in the yard appears to be leaning at a crazy angle – and so it is! We are now in the yard and the reason is clear, the 'Austerity' has left the road and at a very awkward point, on the edge of the track up to the coaling stage. One of the shed staff peers somewhat dubiously at 'WD' Class 2-8-0 No 90254. Working on the ex-Southern Railway metals when new to our railway system, it came north in 1951, initially to Agecroft. A move east to Farnley Junction came in 1956 before nine years of serving other sheds in the Leeds area and a further shift eastwards, to York in December 1965 and West Hartlepool ten months later. Withdrawal was on 25 February 1967 – nearly five months before this shot – and presumably, therefore, it was being moved around the yard before being sent for scrap. Certainly, as betrayed by the open smokebox door, there is no sign of a recent fire with no ash inside the box. *MJS*

Above **Leeds:** Despite the accelerating decline in steam operation, the roundhouse at Leeds (Holbeck) shed was still in regular use. On 1 July there is plenty of steam in view as, from left to right, the turntable is faced by Class '4' 2-6-0 No 43076, Class '8F' 2-8-0 48158 (This loco was made famous back in the 1950's by Hornby choosing to use this number on their 3 rail model - one of your authors still has his!), 'Black 5' Class 4-6-0 Nos 44943 and 45219. The '8F' and the two ''Black 5's'' were all allocated to Holbeck at the date of this view and were withdrawn within a month of each other, between October and November 1967. By comparison, No 43076 was a Royston engine here but would come to Holbeck officially two weeks later; it then saw a transfer to Low Moor (Bradford) – and immediate withdrawal! – on 9 September. New in October 1950 from Darlington Works, it was cut up at Cashmore's scrapyard in Great Bridge, Birmingham in February 1968. *MJS*

Below **Sunderland:** The sheds of the northeast were a mix of ex-LMS and ex-LNER locations, betraying both the rivalry of yesteryear and the shift in regional boundaries over the years. Sunderland was proudly NER in conception and existence, being a parent depot at the birth of British Railways and coded 54A. With changes in thinking, its sphere of influence was diluted in October 1958, by a move to within that of Gateshead and its code becoming 52G. Taking diesels under its wing as a depot from June 1963, it closed as a fully functioning shed with the end of steam on 1 September 1967. Seen on 1 July, just two months from this date, 'K1' Class 2-6-0 No 62012 was not built until August 1949, under the aegis of BR, but had a distinctly LNER lineage. Standing in Sunderland shed's yard, its deceptive appearance of hauling coaches is the focus of attention of visiting Thurmaston Railway Society members. It had been withdrawn six weeks before this view. *MJS*

Above **Wakefield:** Later in the day on 1 July, the enthusiasts of the Thurmaston Railway Society have reached Wakefield shed, one of those formerly under the control of the LMS. This shed was ever a delight to visit, as it had a constantly fluctuating array of home and visiting locomotives, of varying regional types and ages. On this day, a month after official closure, two ex-LMS engines stand on the scrap line with two 'Austerities', whilst outside the shed stand two 'Standard 9Fs'. Originally built by the L&YR, in 1893, it held ten roads, with a turntable in the yard close to the coal stage topped by a water tank, seen on the right of this view. The shed roof seen here was a 1956 louvre style replacement of the original northlight pattern. *MJS*

THIS DOOR FOR EMERGENCY USE ONLY
TO OPEN LIFT HANDLE

Below **West Hartlepool:** We are back at West Hartlepool on 1 July and the dilapidation of the shed is even more apparent in this view, with the roof rapidly disappearing! The foreman crosses the tracks outside the shed, obviously with no interest in a very clean looking Enthusiast Roger Thwaites, camera in hand. 'WD' Class 2-8-0 No 90061 is in steam outside the shed, completing the virtual monopoly of this type on the shed on this day. Originally MoD 0837, No 90061 served a number of sheds in the northeast, including Darlington, Hull (Dairycoates) and (Springhead), Wakefield and, finally, West Hartlepool. Coming to the latter in December 1966, the end came fourteen days after this view, on 15 July. *MJS*

and Springhead (1 December 1958). Sadly, however, the city was never to enjoy fast, direct services to London, with the populace forced to "…travel at sedate and moderate speeds at long intervals." Freight was the main breadwinner for the area from the earliest times and was thus until the end of steam in this year. Many and varied were the multitude of trains entering and leaving the city, marshalling yards and docks, in addition to the numerous trip freights and shunting movements and provided full occupation for the dwindling number of steam locomotives still at work in 1967. The majority at the end were ex-WD 'Austerities', to be replaced by diesels and the new D95xx shunters. These latter, however, were to be short-lived, finding their work disappearing virtually as they were being built! Beeching wielded his axe from 1964 onwards and, forty years on, the city's railway system is a shadow of its former self.

Though there was barely six months left of steam in the northeast, February saw 72 steam locomotives recorded at Wakefield shed – including 32 'Austerities' – and 41 at Leeds (Holbeck) and 2 March had 'K1' Class 2-6-0 No 62044 in some trouble at the head of a 500-ton coal train between Billingham and Port Clarence; but a sign of the times was epitomised by there being 45 locos awaiting cutting at Draper's yard in Hull during March, including a number of '9Fs' and 'V2' Class 2-6-2 No 60831. March also saw 'Jubilee' Class 4-6-0 No 45675 *Hardy* working York-Hull trains; an immaculate 'K1' Class 2-6-0 No 62005 travel to Durham to heat the Royal Train (!); a very rare appearance of 'B1' Class 4-6-0 No 61238 *Leslie Runciman* at the head of a ballast train on the York to Darlington main line – a stretch of line that was virtually steam free by this time; and Class '2' 2-6-2T No 41241 and '1F' Class 0-6-0T No 41708 delivered to the K&WVR.

Further rationalisation in the region came on 17 May, when Leeds City assumed responsibility for all passenger workings in the city, with Central station closing. A century earlier, six railway companies had operated from five different stations but, as the companies disappeared through the various amalgamations, not least the Grouping of 1923, progressive efforts were made to concentrate services into fewer stations, to nominally provide better facilities for passengers, but also to save money. A certain amount of expenditure has had to be made with this latest move, however, with three new chord connections installed to direct traffic into City station. Thus, 133 years of history – starting with the first station at Marsh Lane opening in 1834 – has come to an end. Conceived in 1960, the 'new' station had 12 platforms and included a 12-storey office block, City House. Forty years on and the site has seen more major investment and change, to bring it into the needs and expectations of the 21st century. A single central control signalbox was also provided, handling 520 routes over 47 miles of track and replacing 17 manually operated boxes. In addition, to complete the transformation, a new carriage cleaning and maintenance facility was to be sited adjacent to Neville Hill DMU depot.

Yet more lost lines around the regions

London Midland Region

M 37706 M
ELEPHANT VAN
REPORT TO TRAFFIC P.S. CREWE
LOAD 9 TONS DISTRIBUTED

1967 LINE CLOSURES

Date	From	To	Passenger/Goods
2 January	Derby Midland	Sheffield Midland	*Local Passenger*
	Nottingham Mid.	Sheffield Midland	*Local Passenger*
6 March	Derby Midland	Manchester Central	*Local Passenger*
	Sheffield Midland	Manchester Central	*Local Passenger*
4 September	Grantham	Nottingham Victoria	*Passenger*
5 November	Rockferry	Birkenhead	*Closed*

Continues on next page

Steam was also still finding work in May, but in ever fewer numbers. The Stanlow-Leeds oil train still utilised a double-headed working on the outwards journey; '9F' Class 2-10-0 Nos 92116 and 90404 were active around Goole, the latter hauling dead 'Jubilee' 4-6-0s Nos 45565 *Victoria*, 45694 *Bellerophon* and 45739 *Ulster*; while 'Q6' Class 0-8-0 No 63395 (on a coal train), 'K1' Class 2-6-0 No 62060 (on minerals) and 'Q6' Class 0-8-0 No 63426 were recorded at Gateshead within minutes of each other. 'WD' Class 2-8-0 No 90458 was hauling ex-LMR locos to Draper's scrapyard in Hull in June; mineral trains around Newcastle were largely steam operated, mostly by 'Q6', 'K1', 'J27' and 'Austerity' locomotives; the daily Royston-Goole freights were still steam hauled, but in this month diesels had replaced steam at Goole shed; 'Q6' Class 0-8-0 No 63395 was under repair at Sunderland (!); 'B1' Class 4-6-0 No 61306 was one of the last of its class still in steam, along with Nos 61030 and 61337; and, amazingly, 'A4' Class 4-6-2 No 60019 *Bittern* was used on two days in mid July on freight and parcels trains on the main line between York and Newcastle, although withdrawn!

Right and above: **Memories are made of this...** *Lest we forget!* Steam by 1967 was an endangered species - but there were many specialist services that would also soon disappear. The elephant van was one of many items of rolling stock to become extinct!

August saw 'Jubilee' Class 4-6-0 No 45593 *Kolhapur* handle a relief 'Thames-Clyde Express' north out of Leeds; 'Jubilee' Class 4-6-0 No 45562 *Alberta* on the last 10.17 Leeds-Glasgow train (as far as Carlisle); 'K1' Class 2-6-0 No No 62005 on a Tees Yard-York Dringhouses Yard goods; and 'J27' Class 0-6-0 No 65894 hauled one of the last steam workings in the North East on 8 September, a working to Silksworth Colliery on the last day of this branch, complete with large star and 'North Eastern Steam Farewell' headboard. Steam clung on around the ex-LMR stamping ground at Leeds for a few more weeks, but 1 October saw the end on the Leeds-Bradford route and the final curtain fell.

1967 LINE CLOSURES				
Date	**From**	**To**	**Passenger/Goods**	
30 January	Bodmin Road	Padstow	*Passenger*	***Western Region***
2 October	Coleford	Parkend	*Passenger*	
9 October	Yeovil Town	Yeovil Hendford Goods	*Closed*	
4 December	Totnes	Totnes Quay	*Closed*	
4 December	Exmouth	Exmouth Dock	*Closed*	
6 March	Harrogate	Northallerton	*Passenger*	***North Eastern Region***
6 March	Dairycoates East	St. Andrews Fish Dock	*Closed*	
2 January	Wakefield (Kirkgate)	Pontefract (Monkhill)	*Passenger*	***Eastern Region***
6 March	March	St. Ives (Cambs.)	*Closed*	
2 January	Barassie	Kilmarnock (No 2)	Passenger	***Scottish Region***
4 September	Perth (Stanley Jct.)	Aberdeen (Kinnaber Jct)	Passenger	
6 November	Blackstone Jct	Linwood Goods	Closed	

Right **West Hartlepool:**
Determined to again be included in the shot, Roger Thwaites has his 'ABC Combined' in hand to check the numbers of locos on shed. Still at West Hartlepool on 1 July, 'Q6' Class 0-8-0 No 63397 stands idle and out of steam. Nominally still active, it would be withdrawn on 15 July. Built at Darlington at the end of WWI, to a Raven design by the LNER, it was a very loyal engine, serving just West Hartlepool for most of its BR life. Sadly, it was not to be preserved, unlike its sister No 63395. *MJS*

Locoshed closures by region **1967**

London Midland Region
Eastern Region
North Eastern Region
Scottish Region
Southern Region
Western Region

1967 SHED CLOSURES			
Date	**Code**	**Name**	**Steam/Closed**
6 November	5B	Crewe South	*Closed*
7 August	5C	Stoke on Trent	*Closed*
5 June	6A	Chester	*Closed*
6 November	6C	Birkenhead	*Steam*
2 October	8B	Warrington Dallam	*Closed*
4 November	8F	Wigan Springs Br.	*Steam*
19 June	8G	Sutton Oak	*Closed*
? March	17A	Derby	*Closed*
6 March	21A	Saltley	*Steam*
3 April	24G	Skipton	*Closed*
12 June	27B	Aintree	*Closed*
? June	50A	York	*Steam*
24 June	50B	Hull Dairycoates	*Steam*
8 May	50D	Goole	*Closed*
17 September	51C	West Hartlepool	*Closed*
28 May	52F	Blyth South	*Closed*
9 September	52F	Blyth North	*Closed*
17 September	52G	Sunderland	*Steam*

Above Croes Newydd: Shed closures continued apace during 1967, as can be seen from the adjacent list. Two of these were Birkenhead and Croes Newydd. Both had the distinction of being coded '6C' – the former until 9 September 1963, when it was transferred away from Chester control and diverted to Liverpool, becoming '8H' – but it is the latter's emblem that '5700' Class 0-6-0PT No 9610 is wearing on its smokebox when seen on shed in 1966. The driver seems to be enjoying some joke with the photographer, as he poses for his portrait by Croes Newydd coaling stage. Wolverhampton, Bristol and Wrexham were its main stomping grounds, ending up at Croes Newydd in Janaury 1960. The end was on 6 October 1966. The shed itself was coded CNYD leading up to Nationalisation, becoming 84J (under Wolverhampton's jurisdiction), then 89B from 1 January 1961 (under a new Shrewsbury region) and finally 6C when placed in the BR(MR) realm from 9 September 1963. Built in the triangle of lines at Croes Newydd Junction in 1902, it closed on 5 June 1967. *MJS collection*

1967 SHED CLOSURES Continued

Date	Code	Name	Steam/Closed
9 September	52H	Tyne Dock	Closed
2 October	55A	Holbeck	Closed
? January	55B	Stourton	Closed
30 April	55F	Manningham	Closed
2 February	55G	Huddersfield	Closed
3 June	56A	Wakefield	Closed
? April	56D	Mirfield	Closed
2 October	56F	Low Moor	Closed
18 March	61B	Ferryhill	Steam
? April	62A	Thornton Junction	Closed
1 May	62B	Dundee Tay Bridge	Closed
1 May	62C	Dunfermline	Closed
14 May	63A	Perth	Steam
1 May	64A	St. Margarets	Closed
1 May	66A	Polmadie	Steam
1 May	66B	Motherwell	Closed
2 February	66E	Carstairs	Steam
1 May	66F	Beattock	Steam
1 May	67A	Corkerhill	Steam
9 July	70A	Nine Elms	Closed
7 July	70C	Guildford	Closed
9 July	70G	Salisbury	Closed
9 July	71A	Eastleigh	Closed
9 July	71B	Bournemouth	Closed
9 July	71G	Weymouth	Closed
6 March	84B	Oxley	Closed
6 November	89A	Shrewsbury	Steam
5 June	89B	Croes Newydd	Closed

55A – Leeds (Holbeck)
D2081, D33, D42, D5270, D32, D5179, D174, D1763, D1931, D1505, D35, D5172, 45562 *Alberta*, 45027, 44826, 45273, 45697 *Achilles*, 45593 *Kolhapur*, 45424, 42152, 44828, 92084, 92017, 45080, 42145, 42072, 45208, D3658, D2325, 48104, 44852, D3653, D2249, D2162, 43076, 48158, 44943, D3656, D2092, 45219, 44896, 48283, D2160, 43130, 48542, 48399, 92106, 42689, 44882, 44853, 92165, 45675 *Hardy*, 44993, D2267

56A Wakefield
90047, 92211, 90397, 90363, 90236, 48265, 90654, 90300, 90404, 90396, 90160, 90409, 42236, 44695, 48466, 42235, 42196, 48159, 48075, 42149, 90650, 45647* *Sturdee*, 42267, 90429, 92030, 92065, 92150, 90233, 44946, 90625, 90610, 42287, 42650, 90617, 90362, 45211, 42699, 48157, 42269, 43077, 43098, 42052, 43140, 48123, 45079, 92205, 92215, 61115, 92206, 92006, 90407, 90678, 90620, 92135

* - engines obviously in store. Many of the others were no doubt in the same state, for example at Wakefield, but they were not so obvious!

A Grand Day Out
A spotting trip around the North East on 1 July 1967 – a snapshot of the position with just weeks to go – by one of your authors. 275 locos recorded and 32 'cops'!

52F(S) – South Blyth
D5169, 65813, D6896, D6902

52F(N) – North Blyth
D2315, 62027, 43000, 43137, 43117, 43123, 43055, 43050, D2055, 43071*, 62062*, 65823*, D6873, 65885*, D6831, 65834*, 65861*, 43138*, 43048*, 62057*, 43012*, 43101

52H – Tyne Dock
90361, 90370, 63366, 90382, 62025, D2329, 65795, 62050, 62060, 62007, D5108, D5110, D5107, D2047, D3322, D2050, 65860, 62005, 58, 90200, D5104, D8597, D5111, 63455, 63431, 63387, 63344, 62023, 63429, 63426

52G – Sunderland
65804, 65811, 65855, 65892, 65882, 65789, 65894, 65817, 65880, 90321, 90698, 90056, 90009, 63436, 63437, 63346, 65812, 62012, 63395, D2165, D3242, D6825, 62011, 90112, 65833, D3679

51C – West Hartlepool
90347, 90074, 90695, 62041, 62045, 90677, D5165, 90254, 90339, 90459, 90116, 90210, 90135, 90434, 90061, 90230*, 62048*, 63397*, 63421*, 90588*, 620418, D2099, D3672, 43015, 63407, D2076, 43070, D2205, 63394, D2070, D2586, D2588, D2594, D2591, 63435, D5164, D173, D5185

50A – York
D275, D256, D3076, D2244, D2066, D250, D272, D1894, D8301, D8308, D8305, D5154, D8312, 61337*, 61012* *Puku*, 61019* *Nilghai*, 62001*, 77012*, 77002*, 61030* *Nyala*, 61021* *Reitbok*, D8311, 61123, 61189 *Sir William Gray*, 62065, D168, D2270, D2248, D2262, D2204, D2062, D2063, D8303, D2151, D2340, D2273, D2265, D8309, D2309, D2075, D2158, D2112, D3076, D1980, D5627, 60019 *Bittern*, D9011 *The Royal Northumberland Fusiliers*, D1991

Opposite page **Carnforth:** Coaling towers as built by the LMS may have been concrete monstrosities in some eyes, but they were feats of engineering and imagination. Coal wagons hauled up the side and the coal fed by gravity to waiting tenders/bunkers, they were a 'living' piece of the steam era. This example at Carnforth was a classic example. On 3 August 1968, 'Black 5' 4-6-0 No 45231 ekes out the last hours of BR life, after serving many sheds up and down the WCML over the years. It came to Carnforth on 11 May 1968 and was withdrawn officially 7 September, a month after the end of steam on BR. Happily preservation beckoned and a move to the Great Central Railway at Loughborough followed and in 2006 celebrated its 70th birthday. *MJS*

1968

Farewell to Steam
The final curtain!

For those keen to see how this final year – the annus horribilis for the steam railway enthusiast – compared, it was pleasing to see the number of closures again reduce, this time from 220 to 207, perhaps responding to the apparent change of heart within Government. 1968 may have had less than eight months with steam still operating on BR in daily routines, but that did not lessen the interest in those operations and to the end, steam did not go out with a whimper!

The year began, however, with sad news on another front. On 5 January, a cross-country DMU from Cardiff to Birmingham collided with an electric loco-hauled Manchester-Euston express near Smethwick Rolfe station, due to a signalman's error. Fortunately, no-one was

> MIDLAND RAILWAY.
> **NOTICE.**
> PRIVATE FOOTPATH ONLY.
> TRESPASSERS WILL BE
> PROSECUTED.
> BY ORDER.

Above **Knighton North Junction:** The Gricer's worst nightmare - Trainspotters would pass such signs at their peril! Often found at the entrance to loco sheds such signs, if passed without an official pass, clearly defined permission, or accompanied by a member of staff could result in an uncomfortable meeting with authority! *H. Gamble*

Main picture **Rose Grove:** Enthusiasts swarm like ants around Rose Grove. Looking across the shed yard, '8F' Class 2-8-0 No 48393 is one of a number still in steam on 3 August 1968 the penultimate day. Having been a hard worker around the East Midlands for much of its life, the 8F moved to Lostock Hall in November 1966 and to Rose Grove seven months later. 7 September was its official withdrawal date. Rose Grove shed, on the north side of the line, west of the station, opened for the L&YR in 1899 and other than being re-roofed in 1947, was unchanged thereafter until closure on 5 August 1968. The site later became part of the M65! *MJS*

killed, though 51 passengers were injured, but only two needing to be detained in hospital. Fortune was not so kind, the following day, however, when on 6 January, the 11.30 Manchester Piccadilly-Euston express, travelling at around 70mph, ploughed into a police-escorted transporter lorry at Hixon level crossing, between Stoke and Colwich in Staffordshire. A 125-ton transformer was catapulted 20ft by the impact and the electric locomotive and leading carriages all left the track. Eleven died, including three in the engine's cab. Preliminary enquiries indicated that procedures for abnormal loads were not properly carried out, with no telephone call made to the nearest signalman at Colwich, but there were still calls for an inquiry into the operation of half-barriers at crossings. The line was not re-opened until 15 January and then with a 15mph restriction over the crossing.

The boat service from Fishguard - Rosslare, previously operating at night, was switched to an afternoon, 14.00 departure, to connect with the 08.00 boat train departure from Paddington and during the year it was increased to six days a week from three; an all-year-round hovercraft service between Portsmouth Harbour and Ryde Pier Head was

Lostock Hall What BR steam sheds were all about and just what perhaps cannot be wholly recreated by today's preservationists, no matter how hard they try. On the last day, 4 August, the shed yard at Lostock Hall is full of locos in steam, locos that will work no more, out of picture to the right and an influx of diesels, including what would become Classes 08, 25 and 50. The two steam engines on the left are 'Black 5' 4-6-0 Nos. 45305 and 45212, both readied for their part in the final 'celebrations' and happily preserved subsequently. The former seemed to change abode virtually every year but always on or near the WCML, finishing up at Lostock Hall, whereas No 45212 was a long time servant at Fleetwood before moving to Carnforth in October 1964. There were four moves between that date and the end of steam (including one back to Carnforth for three months in 1965), switching between Liverpool and Carlisle before finally arriving at Lostock Hall. New from Armstrong Whitworth in November 1935, as LMS No 5212, its first shed allocation was to Low Moor; and it

received its BR number in October 1948. After withdrawal following the demise of steam, it escaped the cutter's torch, to find preservation on the Keighley & Worth Valley Railway, arriving there in October 1968. Two years its junior, No 45305 was new from Armstrong Whitworth of Newcastle in 1937 and its home was Keighley & Worth Valley Railway early on but has more latterly been at the GCR. Initially sold to scrap merchants Albert Drapers and Sons Ltd. of Hull, the owner of the scrapyard, A.E. Draper, saved the engine as it was the cleanest engine in the yard! The locomotive is still owned by the scrapyard but is looked after by the *5305 Locomotive Association*, who restored it to original LMS livery for steaming in 1976. In 1984, No 5305 was named *Alderman A E Draper* by the Mayor of Hedon, Bill Tong. A.E. Draper was twice Mayor of Hedon and the Hedon coat of arms is on the nameplates; however, for reasons of authenticity, the engine does not always carry these nameplates. *MJS*

introduced by British Rail Hovercraft Ltd, with a speed of 35 knots, more than three times that of a conventional ferry; and a new ship entered operation on the Stranraer-Larne crossing. Introduced for the Irish Sea services of Caledonian Steam Packet Co Ltd, the *Antrim Princess* was capable of 21 knots, weighed 3,600 tons and had accommodation for 1,200 passengers and 170 cars – or a mix of commercial vehicles and cars.

On the locomotive front, *Kestrel,* now numbered HS4000, was handed over to BR at Marylebone station on 29 January, following which it ran a demonstration trip to Princes Risborough and back. It was originally intended to run on the ECML. The same day saw the opening of Millbrook Freightliner Terminal in Southampton, with the first train to leave being the 1739 to Stratford, in East London, where through portions were detached for hitching to Leeds and Stockton trains. Services to other parts of the UK were added during the year. Elsewhere on the loco front, Tebay shed's 'Standard Class 4' 4-6-0s, employed on banking duties, were replaced by type '1' diesels on 1 January; 'Jubilee' Class 4-6-0 No 45593 *Kolhapur* was bought from BR by *7029 Clun Castle Ltd*; on 15 January, there were 30 engines recorded on Rose Grove shed, including 13 in steam; Stoke shed lost its last four steam locomotives – 'Standard' Class 4 4-6-0 Nos 75046, 75047, 75052 and 75071 – on 12 January; Leicester (Midland) shed – ex-15C – became a centre for preservation, with the roundhouse containing MR 4-4-2 No 118 (LMS No 673),

MR 2-4-0 No 158A, '7F 'Class' 0-8-0 No 49395, 'O1' Class 2-8-0 No 63601, 'V2' Class 2-6-2 No 60800 *Green Arrow* and '4F' Class 0-6-0 No 44027; 10001, second of the 'LMS twins' Co-Co diesels, was cut up at Cox & Danks Ltd's yard at North Acton; and all five of the North British A1A-A1A 'Warships' – D600-605 – were withdrawn as being 'life-expired' after only ten years! Destined to be the only steam locomotives still on BR's books after August, the three VoR narrow gauge engines were also the only steam locos to wear the new blue 'Corporate' livery.

Brunel's Royal Albert Bridge, carrying the railway over the River Tamar – already well over 100 years old! – was scheduled to be strengthened to carry heavier trains, by the addition of 24 steel diagonal bracing 'ties'. In an attempt to reduce costs, conductor/guards were introduced to the Minehead-Taunton services from 26 February, but with booking offices remaining open at both ends of the run. Buxton shed closed to steam on 4 March, with the last loco to leave in steam being 8F Class 2-8-0 No 48744 on the previous day, a Sunday; meanwhile, a week earlier, 32 steam engines were recorded at Bolton shed, with at least 20 in steam, and 48 at Carnforth, with 14 in steam; in contrast,

Main picture **Carnforth:** We have previously seen 'Black 5' 4-6-0 No 45342 at Carnforth on *page 5*, when the improved appearance of the loco in that picture was commented upon. The wholly disreputable sight of it some months earlier can be readily judged in this view from 15 April 1968. Externally it looks as dispensed with as the other steam locos dumped in the storage sidings at the back of shed – one without chimney! – but as already seen, it lived to fight another day. Another servant of Leicester (Midland) shed – to 4 December 1954 – it also had spells at Leicester (GC) shed from June to September 1960 and January 1963 to June 1964. Mean times, it was at Saltley, Bedford, Kentish Town, Derby, Woodford Halse, Annesley and, finally, Carnforth from, 3 July 1965. Thereafter it became one of the increasing number to feel the oxy-acetylene's bite. *MJS*

Right **Patricroft:** In the closing days, locos were stored all over the northwest and Patricroft shed had its fair share. Most of the inhabitants at this time were stored inside the shed buildings and one such is seen here on 2 August. 'Standard' Class 5 4-6-0 No 73138 stands with 'sister' No 73135 as one of several of the Class on shed this day, obviously not about to work again, with its connecting rods securely fastened to the high running plate. One of 30 of the later built examples fitted

1968
THE END
OF STEAM
2008

with Caprotti valve gear post-1956, it was new on 1 December of that year, going straight to Holyhead, to haul the North Wales Coast trains to/from Crewe. Within two months it had moved to Leicester (Midland) – staying there for two years – after which it remained a MML loco until the move to Patricroft on 6 June 1964. It was withdrawn on 18 May 1968 and cut up some time afterwards. *MJS*

Patricroft: Don't believe a word of it! The camera may not lie, but the scrawled chalk messages do, for this is not 'Britannia' Class 4-6-2 No 70036 *Bodicea* or 'Castle' Class No 5054 *The Earl of Ducie*, both of which were once gleaming express engines, but the far more humble Stanier 8F 2-8-0 heavy freight locomotive! Presumably, the 'V' is for victory and not some other message; and 'Patricroft Flyer' an attempt at bestowing some dignity on the abandoned loco. The actual persona is No 48390, a Derby engine for many years before it shifted allegiance to Manchester and Heaton Mersey shed on 4 March 1961. The last move, to Patricroft, was on 29 January 1966 and, as will not be surprising, it had already been withdrawn at the date of this photograph, since 18 May. The sun shines brightly but does nothing to lift the general malaise. *MJS*

20 were at Normanton, all withdrawn and including 'Jubilee' Class 4-6-0s No 45562 *Alberta* and No 45697 *Achilles*, together with 'B1' Class 4-6-0 No 61306. On the other side of the coin, the new Wigan TMD was opened on 3 April, replacing the old Springs Branch steam shed that closed the previous December. With the Mayor of Wigan present, the formalities were performed by R L E Lawrence, Chairman & General Manager of the London Midland Region. At 282ft long and 137ft wide, it was built to hold 12 'Type 4' locos on three roads, with illuminated pits and was the only depot of its kind at the time on the 114 miles between Crewe and Carlisle, provided as part of BR's modernisation programme for the region.

As the end of steam approached, BR's Annual Report revealed the parlous state of the railway's affairs, despite the elimination of thousands of locomotives, countless numbers of

Above **Lostock Hall:** Another bedraggled, work weary loco that had not seen an oily rag for some considerable time! On 15 April, '8F' Class 2-8-0 No 48646 is still in service at Lostock Hall and, presumably, serviceable despite appearances, but will not have too much opportunity to show its mettle, as it only has three months of life left. Withdrawal came on 13 July after a period of 17 months at the depot, with previous homes including Wellingborough, Canklow, Rugby, Bletchley, Birkenhead and Saltley. Its fellow class members line up behind it and all will suffer similar fates. *MJS*

stations, sheds, staff and practices and renewed efforts to woo passengers and freight back to rail. The results for 1967 showed an increase in deficit to £153m from £135m the previous year and the only 'bright spots' were the development of Merry-go-Round and Freightliner services. Overall, there was around an 8% drop in ton miles and 2% in passenger journeys – not a good sign for a Government still battling to drive BR into profit! The signing of a new contract to transship car bodies from Linwood, Renfrewshire to Coventry, for Rootes Motors Scotland Ltd; the inauguration of high-capacity sea container services between Harwich and Zeebrugge; and trains of Scotch whisky from Edinburgh, for Arthur Bell & Sons Ltd and bound for Bremen, Germany, were but small steps in the right direction. The Ministry of Transport was forecasting 125mph trains in five years and 150mph in ten!!!! We were not the only country reducing the rail mileage, as Italian State Railways wanted to close 2,870 miles, a quarter of the entire system! As the summer wore on, steam enthusiasts travelled the country in large numbers, grabbing what experiences they could and they also had some *gratifying news*, that the first diesels had arrived at Dai Woodham's yard at Barry for scrap – D6122 (from Scotland!) and D600/D601 from Laira.

1968
40
THE END
OF STEAM
YEARS
2008

August dawned all too suddenly and with it came **THE END!** The Grim Reaper had succeeded in his attempts to eradicate the 18,500 steam locomotives in existence at the time of the 1955 Modernisation Plan, plus the 500 built subsequently to 1960. Bearing in mind that some of the modern types were anticipated to have "a useful life of some forty years", the end was sooner than many imagined possible. It was little comfort that steam was being progressively withdrawn throughout the World, or that preservation schemes were springing up with some regularity – a case in point being the K&WVR, which opened on 29 June. The cry that these restorationists were 'spreading the jam too thin' and that many schemes were doomed to failure was soon voiced – and has been regularly ever since – but in 2008, there seems to be no end to the process, with many lines going from strength to strength, extending their route mileage and even, in parts, re-attaching themselves to the main lines!

'**B**lack 5' 4-6-0 No 45212 hauled one of the last steam-hauled down trains – the 20.50 Preston - Blackpool – with 'sister' loco No 45318 on the 21.25 Preston - Liverpool on the evening of 3 August; and then, in the early hours of Sunday, 4 August, No 45212 shunted the sleeping cars from the 23.45 Euston-Preston into the bay at the destination and it was all over! Or nearly!

Carnforth: The date is 3 August 1968, your photographer's 25th birthday. As a sort of birthday treat, just one day before the 'total eclipse' of steam on BR, two Stanier 'Black 5' 4-6-0s stand under Carnforth's 'twin towers'. In the distance, others are stored, but these two are clinging to life, literally in the case of No 45342, right, for, as we have seen on *page 5*, it will be moved from this location to the scrap line and allowed to die. As we have also seen, on *page 110*, its companion, No 45231, defied the cutter's torch to achieve preservation and restoration and latterly to celebrate its 70th birthday on the current GCR. The fireman, left, calls to his mate on No 45342, with his hand up to his mouth to, presumably, hide some confidential statement! *MJS*

The Sunday was to see various privately organised 'Farewell to Steam' specials. A SLS special from Birmingham employed 'Black 5' 4-6-0 Nos 44874 and 45017; another tour was graced with 'Britannia' Class 4-6-2 No 70013 *Oliver Cromwell* leading 'Black 5' 4-6-0 No 44781; and, ringing the changes completely, a RCTS train originating at Euston had '8F' Class 2-8-0 No 48476 and 'Standard' Class 5 4-6-0 No 73069 at its head. 'Black 5' 4-6-0 No 45156, formerly *Ayrshire Yeomanry*, hauled a GC Enterprises tour; 'Black 5' 4-6-0 Nos. 45390 and 45025 had a LCGB tour that had started at St Pancras; and '8F' Class 2-8-0 No 48773 and 'Black 5' 4-6-0 No 44781 double-headed a leg of another.

The very last official standard gauge train to be steam hauled was 'The 15-Guinea Special' of 11 August, from Liverpool (Lime Street) to Carlisle, via Manchester (Victoria), hauled variously by 'Black 5' Class 4-6-0 Nos. 45110, 44781, 44871, and 'Britannia' Class 4-6-2 No 70013 *Oliver Cromwell*. 420 passengers paid the not-insignificant fare and enjoyed a cold lunch with champagne, as well as the joys of the journey and the occasion. Wearing '1T57' special board, No 45110 left Liverpool at 0910 and ran to Manchester, where No 70013 *Oliver Cromwell* took over for the run to Carlisle. Photographic stops were made along the way, including Rainhill, site of the 1829 locomotive trials. No 44871 and 44781 double-headed the return working to Manchester and No 45110 back to Liverpool. The 'Britannia' followed light engine as far as Lostock Hall shed. It then made its way, under its own steam (!), to Norwich on 12th, from where it was passed to preservation at Bressingham Gardens. The fascinating story of how 'Black 5' No 45110 came to be saved can be found on *pages 132-139*. The month concluded with the 125th Anniversary of the opening of Swindon Works, but without steam on display!

Right **Rose Grove:** The countdown to the end and the number of steam operated services forever dwindled. As we have seen in previous years, the 'end days' saw a decline in the attention to detail in the maintenance of those locomotives still nominally in working order. Numberplates, works plates, shedplates all 'mysteriously' disappeared and the external condition of most of the final workhorses certainly left a lot to be desired! A case in point is the grimy 'Standard' Class 9F, bereft of any form of identifiable persona, climbing away from Rose Grove on 4 May, with a Saturdays Only parcels duty. Note the tall coaling tower of Rose Grove shed in the background; and the embankments clear of the tree growth that is so common nowadays. *J K Morton, MJS collection*

Far right **Spring Vale:** Double-headed on a three-coach train and a special at that! On 27 April, 'Standard' Class 5 4-6-0 Nos 73050 and 73069 accelerate away from Spring Vale station, between Blackburn and Bolton, with an unidentified '1Z77' special working. As there is no evidence of recent rain in the area, one can only assume

The railway still continued, of course, after August and change apart from the loss of steam was not lessened. 9 September, for example, witnessed track lifting on the Cambridge-Bedford line; 28 September was the closure date for New England shed, after 115 years of operation; 7 October saw all services to Sheffield transferred to the Midland, bringing an end to the sometimes prestigious services, like 'The Master Cutler', that previously ran to King's Cross; 20 August saw a new Freightliner service exclusively for the use of Ford Motor Co Ltd, between Halewood and Harwich; on 8 September, BR abandoned charging fares on a mileage basis and switched to a more selective system, whereby costs would be based on the quality

that an oily rag has been used on No 73050, in an attempt to smarten it up, whereas its 'sister' appears to be in a more genuinely good condition. Note the differing design of tenders in use by them.

Both locomotives were new from Derby in 1954 – No 73050 in May and No 73069 six months later. '50' went first to Bath (Green Park) shed and stayed there until moving to Bristol (Barrow Road) on 11 August 1962. Various moves saw it, among other places, at Llanelli for a month in the spring of 1964, then two years at Shrewsbury before moves to Agecroft and, finally, Patricroft. After withdrawal on 13 July, just before the very end of steam, it was saved for preservation and a move to the Nene Valley Railway, where it has gained the name of *City of Peterborough*. In contrast, No 73069 was always a LMR loco, being 'owned' by no fewer than eleven different sheds. The first eight years saw it on the MML before a move to the West Midlands in late 1964, Manchester in April 1966 and, finally, Carnforth in July 1968. It survived to the bitter end but not to achieve preservation. *J K Morton, MJS collection*

of service offered and the usage by the public! The route between Princes Risborough and Aynho was singled (to be doubled again 2006 as Project Evergreen and a cost of c£8m!); and John Craig, the last top hatted stationmaster, retired after 48 years service, from Liverpool (in charge of Lime Street, Exchange and Central stations, with 700 staff under him!). On the locomotive front, a new numbering system was announced, to suit computerised accounting records, with diesels reclassified in types from '01' (smallest) to '55' (most powerful) and electrics from '70' (the three ancient ex-Southern engines) to '86' (the WCML main line locomotives). The prefix 'D' on diesel locomotives was also to be abandoned, following the end of steam and the resultant elimination of confusion; 'E' on electrics was to continue! In addition, as part of an all-regional scheme to standardise and rationalise spares, all 'Class 27's' were transferred from the LMR to Scotland, initially allocated to Eastfield; and *Kestrel* was moved to work on the WCML.

The year ended with the announcement and imminent demise of the Taunton-Minehead route and closure of all interim stations! Announcements were also being introduced onto trains, in an attempt to assist passengers with their journey and were generally accepted well; however, the musical intermissions were viewed with much less enthusiasm!

Below **Bolton Shed:** Not exactly like painting the Forth Bridge, but cleaning a standard gauge main line steam locomotive single handedly – and by hand – is no picnic. On a damp and dismal 23 March 'Black 5' 4-6-0 No 45260 is gradually emerging from the patina of dirt, ash and grime on Bolton shed. Even from this view, without venturing any closer, it is obvious why it had become increasingly difficult to recruit young men into service on the steam railway. Cold and dirty as often as not, with only limited

Locos withdrawn in last 5 months of steam in the North West			
Period end	**Shed**	**Steam**	**Diesel**
18 May	Lostock Hall	43019, 43027, 48445	
	Heaton Mersey	44663, 45065, 45190, 45392, 48252, 48322, 48329, 48365, 48471, 48551, 48684	
	Bolton	44664, 44829, 45381, 48702	
	Edge Hill	44711, 44864, 45282, 45284, 48045, 48056, 48124, 48614, 48722	
	Stockport Edgeley	44836, 44855, 44868, 45013, 45027, 48182, 48745	
	Newton Heath	45254, 48533,	D2373
	Speke Junction	45201, 48206, 92054, 92069, 92094, 92218, 92249	
	Patricroft	48325, 48390, 73040, 73128, 73138, 73142, 73157	
	Carnforth	92088	D2390
	Crewe Works		D2176
	Croes Newydd		D2374, D2375
	Springs Branch, Wigan		D2376, D2377, D2379
	Rugby		D2380
	Crewe Diesel Depot		D2384, D2395
	Allerton		D2396
	Carlisle Kingmoor Diesel Depot		D5715, D5718
13 June	Newton Heath	44803, 45411, 48687, 48746	
	Patricroft	45187, 48267, 48282, 48327, 48338, 48374, 48467, 48549	
	Carnforth	45345, 92091, 92118	

Period end	Shed	Steam	Diesel
	Bolton	48380	
	Lostock Hall	48646	
	Rose Grove	48384	
	Toton		D3446, D3448, D3476, D3498
13 July	Lostock Hall	*43106*, 44878, 44942, 45149, 48293, 48546	
	Patricroft	44777, 48033, 48170, 48212, 48491, 73010, **73050**, 73125, 73133, 73134, 73143	
	Newton Heath	44780, 44818, 44845, 44884, 44890, 44891, 44910, 44949, 45076, 45202, 45203, 45255, 45420, 48132, 48321, 48356, 48368, 48369, 48373, 48529, 48612, 48620, 48678	
	Bolton	44802, 44929, 44947, 45046, 45104, 45290, 45312,48026, 48168, 48319, 48392, 48504, 48652, 48692, 48720	
	Carnforth	45209, 45435, 45445, 92077, 92160, 92167	
	Rose Grove	45382, 48115, 48323	

Continued on next page

1968
THE END
OF STEAM
YEARS
2008

cab protection from the elements after hours of preparation for the loco to be ready, was not the most inspiring job description! This 'Black 5' was yet another migrant worker, with no fewer than 18 changes of allocation during the 20 years of BR's existence and serving Derby shed on six different occasions! It was shedded at Bolton as seen here, but then travelled to Lostock Hall on 6 July, after Bolton shed closed its doors on the 1st of the month.

Period end	Shed	Steam	Diesel
	Springs Branch, Wigan		D2214, D2228
	Allerton		D2221
	Toton		D3442, D3450, D3452, D3475, D3482, D3490, D3493, D3495, D3501
10 August	Rose Grove	44690, 44899, 44932, 45096, 45156, 45262, 45287, 45350, 45397, 45447, 48062, 48167, 48191, 48247, 48253, 48257, 48278, 48340, 48348, 48393, 48400, 48410, 48423, 48448, 48476, 48493, 48519, 48665, 48715, 48727, 48730, 48752, *48773*	
	Carnforth	44709, 44735, 44758, 44809, 44874, 44877, 44894, 44897, 44963, 45017, *45025*, 45095, 45134, 45200, 45206, *45231*, 45268, 45310, 45330, 45342, 45390, 45394, 73069, 75009, 75019, 75020, *75027*, 75048	
	Lostock Hall	44713, *44806*, 44816, 44888, 44950, 44971, 45055, 45073, *45212*, 45260, 45269, *45305*, 45318, 45353, 45386, 45388, *45407*, 45444, 48294, 48723, 48765, 48775	

Bolton Shed: With empty sidings, fewer locomotives and wagons peopling the locations, the railway hinterland became increasingly run down and depressed in appearance in the later days of steam. Another view of Bolton on 23 March, shows the loco yard and coaling tower with two more 8Fs latterly abandoned and stored on one of the redundant sidings.

The earliest shed at Bolton had been built by the grandly named Manchester, Bolton & Bury Canal Navigation & Railway Co. in 1838, being a modest two-road dead end facility just to the south of Trinity Street station. Lasting only two years, this was replaced by a three-road building within a triangle of lines slightly further south and, possibly supplementing a one-road shed at the east side of the station; and then the position was totally rationalised by a new shed, on the west side of the line, even further south of Trinity Street in 1874. Brick built with four roads, it was enlarged in 1888 to eight roads within the building; a new roof was in place by the LMS in 1946 and then matters rested until closure in subsequent demolition.

Period end	Shed	Steam	Diesel
	Crewe Diesel		D2208
	Allerton		D2209
	Birkenhead		D2338
	Toton		D3473, D3632
	Colwick		D3625, D3626, D3627, D4064, D4086
7 September (official date, plus for many of the above)	Carnforth	44781, *44871*, *70013 Oliver Cromwell*	
	Lostock Hall	*45110*	
	LMW (Western A C Lines)		E3009
	Birkenhead		D2213
	Crewe Diesel Depot		D2218
	D10 (Preston Division)		D5701, D5702, D5705, D5706, D5707, D5708, D5711, D5712, D5714, D5716, D5717, D5719

Locomotives shown in green italics have been preserved see table on page 139

Below: On 4 August the SLS ran two identical tours – Farewell to steam No1 and Farwell to steam No2! – starting out from Birmingham (New Street) behind electric traction. Diesel took over between Stockport and Manchester Victoria, via Droylesden, before double-headed steam were given the road at Victoria for a roundabout route to Stockport and the tours' final run back to New Street by electric. Running as '1Z78' throughout, tour No1 had 'Black 5' 4-6-0 Nos 44871 and 44894 in charge, to wend their way as Manchester Victoria – Diggle – Huddersfield – Sowerby Bridge – Copy Pit – Blackburn – (via Bolton avoiding line) – Wigan Wallgate – Kirkby – Bootle – Stanley – Rainhill – Barton Moss – Manchester Victoria – Droylesden – Stockport. They are seen during one of the photo opportunities, as they pause for water. *Gerald Adams/MJS collection*

Locoshed closures by region 1968

| London Midland Region |
| Eastern Region |
| North Eastern Region |
| Scottish Region |
| Southern Region |
| Western Region |

1968 SHED CLOSURES

Date	Code	Name	Steam/Closed
6 May	8A	Edge Hill	*Steam*
6 May	8C	Speke Junction	*Closed*
4 March	8E	Northwich	*Steam*
6 May	9B	Stockport Edgeley	*Closed*
4 March	9D	Buxton	*Closed*
4 March	9E	Trafford Park	*Closed*
6 May	9F	Heaton Mersey	*Closed*
1 January	12A	Carlisle Kingmoor	*Closed*
1 January	12F	Workington	*Steam*
1 January	12H	Tebay	*Closed*
5 August	24B	Rose Grove	*Closed*
4 August	24C	Lostock Hall	*Closed*
5 August	24L	Carnforth	*Closed**
1 February	26A	Newton Heath	*Steam*
1 July	26C	Bolton	*Closed*
1 July	26F	Patricroft	*Closed*
1 January	55E	Normanton	*Closed*

* Following closure Camforth Shed became a working museum - *Steamtown Railway Museum* which was open to the public until June 1997. The shed is no longer open to the public being the working maintenance and servicing base for *West Coast Railway Company Ltd*

Bottom left **Rose Grove:** At the opening of 1968, there were just a baker's dozen of sheds still open with steam allocations and Rose Grove was of them and was to play a vital role in satisfying the thirst for steam right up to the end. On 23 March, with still 4+ months to go, there was much work still handled by the depot, mostly by yet more of Stanier's 8Fs. At the head of this short row of engines awaiting their fate, between the turntable and sidewall of the shed building, No 48392 stands in steam and in company of 'Standard' Class 4 4-6-0 No 75032. By far the older of the two and introduced by the LMS, the 8F was a MML based loco until 28 March 1964, when it transferred allegiance to the Manchester area and Stockport (Edgeley) shed. 3½ years later a short move across town to Trafford Park was followed by Lostock Hall (from 9 March 1968) and finally Bolton 21 days later. Thus it is visiting from Lostock Hall when seen at Rose Grove. Withdrawal was before the final curtain, on 13 July. By comparison, No 75032 was new on 11 July 1953, to Bletchley, after which it moved to Llandudno Junction on 26 February 1955. Perambulations around the system off the WCML then followed, with a total of 15 allocations in its life, including four terms at Llandudno, before ending up at Carnforth in January 1968. Withdrawal was even earlier than the 8F, on 24 February, less than fifteen years old and, thus, is out of work when snapped in this row.

Previous page bottom right **Bolton Shed:** Like its contemporary at Carnforth, Bolton was graced with an LMS concrete coaling plant, seen here on 23 March astride the tender of '8F' Class 2-8-0 No 48026. In front, trying to escape capture by the camera, is 'Black 5' 4-6-0 No 45104. Both designed by Stanier, for heavy freight and mixed traffic work respectively, No 48026 was a MR loco at the birth of BR, at 19C (Canklow) but this shed would be redesignated to the ER on 1 February 1958, as 41D. Remaining there until December 1962, Staveley (Barrow Hill) was the next port of call before a transfer back to the MR in 1964. Liverpool and Manchester sheds were the operators there up to withdrawal from Bolton on 13 July. No 45104 by comparison was a MR loco throughout its BR life, predominantly in and around Manchester. Its grim reaper also appeared on 13 July. Note the number of white painted point levers needed to handle the sometimes convoluted movements around the shed yard.

1968 LINE CLOSURES - A selection

Date	From	To	Passenger/Goods
1 January	Oxford	Bletchley	*Passenger*
4 March	Birmingham NS	Derby Midland	*Local Passenger*
	Birmingham NS	Leicester London Rd	*Local Passenger*
	Nottingham Mid	Leicester London Rd	*Local Passenger*
25 March	Stratford-on-Avon	Gloucester Central	*Passenger*
1 July	Matlock	Chinley	*Passenger*
	Manchester Exch.	Huddersfield	*Local Passenger*
1 January	Bedford St Johns	Cambridge	*Passenger*
29 January	Alnmouth	Alnwick	*Closed*
9 September	Dereham	Kings Lynn	*Closed*
1 January	Carbert	Alloa	*Passenger*

Below **Lostock Hall:** Another view of Lostock Hall, this time on the side furthest away from the main line, with an unidentified 'Black 5' in steam but with a wholly incorrect number painted on the smokebox! The legends state: "Goodbye, but not forgotten. 1830-1968" and "10D x 24K". All very well but....what is supposed to be being celebrated, as 1830 has no specific reference here and certainly not to the locomotive or shed! Similarly, whilst 10D was the current code for Lostock Hall at this date, its pre-1963 persona was 24C, not 24K, which was Preston! And with a spurious, non-existent front number, not only is it weird, but also incomprehensible and largely pointless!

Initially sited on the north side of the line, east of Lostock Hall station by the L&YR the first shed closed in 1881. Its replacement was built alongside the southern edge of the station, abutting up to Watkin Lane that crossed the railway complex in the area. Opening on 30 October 1881, it was brick built with a northlight roof pattern and eight roads as a dead end straight shed. Re-roofed in 1953 by BR, it closed immediately after business on this day, 4 August, but remained standing for many years thereafter, initial use being made by the Civil Engineer's Department. *MJS*

The 15-Guinea Special
and the saving of
'Black 5' No 45110 R.A.F. Biggin Hill
By David Porter

Sunday 11 August 1968 As dawn broke, many hundreds of people were heading for one particular location, a landmark, who's name has become synonymous with the City of Liverpool - Lime Street Station. Normally quiet at this hour, on a weekend, except for a few night workers coming off shift, it had the activity that would normally be associated with the height of the weekday rush hour. Meanwhile, vast numbers of spectators, including armies of railway devotees, from all parts of the country, were converging

Left **Bewdley (SVR) 1998:** No 45110 *R.A.F. Biggin Hill is* in fine fettle, and with steam to spare as she awaits departure from Bewdley. The two young admirers like thousands of others have men like David Porter (inset) who cared enough about our heritage to save just a few of these magnificent giants of steam - against all the odds! *PT*

Right **The Fifteen Guinea Special:** A stunning shot captured by Dick Manton on 11 August 1968. 'Black 5' 4-6-0 No 45110 storms through Edge Hill Cutting en-route from Liverpool to Manchester (Victoria) with 1T57 the last official British Rail standard gauge steam hauled train. LMR Divisional Manager and lifelong railwayman Richard Hardy leans out of the cab and keeps a watchful eye as passengers also lean out to savour the full atmosphere. *Dick Manton*

on locations along the 157 miles of line between Liverpool and Carlisle, on the Settle route, via Manchester, and the 'long drag' through Ribblesdale and over Ais Gill. The crowds of onlookers and the cars congesting the roads and the moorland tracks of Cumbria had taken the police and railway authorities completely by surprise, and far exceeded the numbers they had anticipated controlling.

The reason behind all this activity, which had caused traffic jams over a wide area of North West England, was to get a glimpse, and perhaps a never to be repeated photograph, in the brief moments it would take one particular train to pass them by. Diesel and electric locomotives would go about their tasks almost unnoticed. The focal point of attention for the vast crowds was to observe, for what they had been led to believe would be for the last time on a main line, was the sight, the sound and the smell from drifting smoke and steam, that had been a familiar part of the daily scene throughout all their lives, somehow taken for granted, the epitome of harnessed power - the robust, but majestic Steam Locomotive. An enduring cornerstone of everyday life was being eliminated, its permanence so long taken for granted by many generations.

Left **Bridgnorth (SVR):** The Reverend R.C. Hubble dedicates 'Black 5' 4-6-0 No 45110 *R.A.F. Biggin Hill* in the presence of (on his right) Flight Lieutenant A. R. J. Pascall (Biggin Hill); Air Commodores P. M. Brothers, CBE, DSO, DFC (Director of Public Relations) and J. W. Allan, DSO, DFC, AFC, MBIM (Commandant Biggin Hill).

Locomotives still capable of many years of revenue-earning work, had already been dispatched, with undue bureaucratic haste to scrap yards around the country, political aims had been allowed to override common sense in a manner similar to the earlier Beeching axe that desecrated the greatest asset that our Victorian forbears bequeathed

to this country by closing lines, stations and freight yards, that today are desperately needed to relieve our congested and dangerous roads This however was not just another summer's day in August with steam locomotives going about their work on the railways of Britain. To the total anguish of the Steam enthusiasts, and to a great extent, the disbelief of the general public at large, the day that standard gauge, steam traction on BR would end, had finally arrived, there would be no last minute stay of execution, scepticism had given way to realisation, as an unnamed steam locomotive, former LMS Stanier 'Black 5'. Class 5MT. 4-6-0. No 45110 departed precisely on time at ten past nine, with train 1T57.

In the capable hands of Driver John Hart, and Fireman Brian Bradley, both experienced Liverpool Railwaymen from Edge Hill MPD No 45110 stormed out of the station to make a faultless and spirited departure from Lime Street. Hauling a fully loaded 10 coach train of 470 privileged passengers she

was picking up speed, and had power to spare as she passed through Edge Hill station, heading for Manchester Victoria. Spectators were by now occupying every conceivable vantage point along the train's route. Attacking the 1 in 93 incline out of the station with its towering vertical walls, short tunnels and overbridges, and clearing the last of the bridges carrying Tunnel Road at the top of the gradient. The souvenir brochure prepared by British Rail's publicity department gave an historical account of railways from 1825 to 1968, and of particular interest, information on the locomotives selected to work their last main line steam train, first on the list was Stanier 'Black 5'. No 45305, which would haul the train on the first leg of its journey, out of Liverpool, returning from Manchester later in the day to conclude the tour. As the smokebox number plate of No 45110 was almost obscured by a larger than usual board, bearing the train identification code, 1T57, only the bottom of each of the locomotives numerals were visible under the board, which made it impossible to decipher her number.

45110
One of the few

Lostock Hall: We have seen Nos. 45305 and 45212 previously on *page 114*, but they are captured again on 4 August from a slightly different and closer angle at Lostock Hall, with the shed buildings just visible in the background. To the left, dominating the picture, is '8F' Class 2-8-0 No 48493, a survivor to the very end, but not in steam on the very last day and, sadly not one of the greater survivors through preservation. A long time resident of Staveley (Barrow Hill) shed, it transferred to the WCML on 10 November 1962 with a move to Willesden. Thereafter, sheds on or close to the 'Premier Line' remained in control until its eventual arrival at Rose Grove on 11 May 1968. Initially designated 24B by BR in 1948, Rose Grove remained with that code until a massive rethink by BR(MR) on 9 September 1963, when it transferred from Accrington (24A) area authority to being within Carnforth's (10A) domain, as 10F. Devoid of actual front numberplate and shedplate, both have been somewhat crudely been painted onto the smokebox. The niceties of steam operation had long since been dispensed with! *MJS*

Texts for photographs and newspaper articles had already been drafted which included a background on 'Black 5'. No 45305, and it was not until the locomotive began to draw away from the platform, and the smoke and steam that had been enveloping the engine, drifted away, and the onlookers began to realise that a twist of fate had taken a hand, as her cabside number came into view, No 45305, had been replaced, and it was now No 45110 that was at the head of the train, and was destined to be transformed from permanent obscurity - as was to be the fate of many of her class - to historic acknowledgement and importance.

The locomotive originally allocated to haul the train 1T57 on this final journey of British Rail's steam era No 45305, had been declared, 'Unfit to work in traffic', the previous day by Lostock Hall's shrewd and erudite Shedmaster Harold Sedgebeer. Earlier in the week when he received the list of locomotives allocated for the 'Last day turns' he had questioned why No 45110, which had only returned from her annual check in June, had been listed as 'Stand by Locomotive'. He considered her to be the most mechanically sound of all the 'Black 5's in his care, it having worked, providing sterling service, as recently as the first week in August.

Only her appearance left much to be desired, the next 15 hours would however see a total transformation. There were now only a few permanent staff remaining at the depot, and with less than one day to go, the task ahead of them to restore her paintwork to main line standard, was formidable. A call from Harold Sedgebeer, brought volunteers from his many contacts amongst older Locomen, who had worked with him in previous years, but had now retired or been transferred to office posts. These railwaymen from the age of steam, who remained anonymous, on the work sheets, still had a pride in the appearance of their locomotives, and with the limited resources available worked into the night. By morning as Fiftyone-ten left

Lostock Hall for Lime street, a transformation had taken place, Those who may have glanced at her a few days earlier amongst the 30 or so silent locomotives, awaiting departure to scrap yards, would not have considered it were possible; her brasses and motion polished, her paintwork shining from immeasurable applications of diesel oil, and with sufficient dirt removed to revel her London & North Western Railway mixed traffic style livery. No 45110 was a fine example of her class, and a credit to her designer, Sir William Stanier, as she departed at the head of train 1T57.

Twenty minutes after her departure No 45110 was halted for a short while to enable her passengers to detrain and join the large crowd that had gathered at Rainhill, near Newton-le-Willows Lancashire, the site of the legendary 1829 Locomotive trials. Thus acknowledging the location's importance in the history of Railways. A further stop was also made at Parkside as a mark of respect to the Rt. Hon William Huskisson, M.P. a keen supporter of Railways, who was fatally injured at the official opening ceremony of the Liverpool and Manchester Railway, in 1830 when he was struck by Stephenson's locomotive 'Rocket'.

Later in the day, after the train's return to Manchester from Carlisle, during which the passengers had travelled behind three other, now also legendary "Last Day" Locomotives, 'Black 5's No's. 44871 and 44781 (double heading) and 'Britannia' Class No 70013 *Oliver Cromwell.* No 45110 was again attached to the head of the train, which has since become dubbed "BR's Fifteen Guinea Special", to complete the last leg of its now poignant journey from Manchester into Liverpool's Lime Street Station to become the last steam locomotive to haul a scheduled passenger train on British Rail's standard gauge, thus bringing to an end the magnificent era of steam on the railways of Great Britain after 143 years. The enthusiasm of the passengers and the thousands of onlookers had now given way to a silent melancholy acceptance that they were witnessing the last rites of steam, and the focus of their attention the impending demise of 'Black 5' No 45110 at the hands of the cutter's torch, a fate that had already befallen the majority of the 842 Locomotives of her class.

As Fiftyone-ten marked her final departure from the Lime Street station with a long blast on her whistle followed by three thunderous reports, as she ran over fog detonators placed on the

45110

One of the few

Above **Arley:** Hawker Hurricane PZ865, "The Last of the Many", makes a low pass, in salute to restored 'Black 5' No 45110 *R.A.F. Biggin Hill*, at Arley, on the Severn Valley Railway. The Hurricane was the last of 12,540 built in the UK during WW II. *Painting by Ossie Jones © D. Porter (Stafodex)*

track which echoed throughout the station's massive train shed, the majority of the crowds remained until the locomotive had disappeared, obscured by smoke and steam into the tunnels and overbridges that are a feature of the approach to Lime Street station. Only now did the crowds observing this historic occasion gradually drift away, unaware that within a short while, I, having also witnessed these scenes of No 45110 on the late evening television news, in which the commentator unbelievably referred to the locomotive leaving Lime Street and "going straight to the breakers yard", would begin a hectic week of negotiations to endeavour to preserve the locomotive and secure a permanent future for her.

Every piece of the jigsaw was unplanned, but as each part fell into place, a sequence of events unfolded, that was in the best traditions of Railway Preservation, brinkmanship and individual determination, against bureaucratic indifference!

45110's future was Hanging by a thread ....

A series of phone calls late that evening, and into the early hours of Monday morning with a sympathetic contact on the British Railways Board, established that No 45110 had returned to the MPD at Lostock Hall, near Preston, after leaving Lime Street that evening. It was also confirmed that she was one of a batch of steam locomotives designated to be sold to a Midlands scrap merchant. However, there was a chance as the merchant's tender had not yet been received at the BR offices in Preston, and if his papers failed to arrive by the morning of Monday the 12 August, a five day moratorium might be granted, on the locomotive, providing I deposited a signed 'Letter of Intent to Purchase', at their offices by 3.00 pm that afternoon, which could only contain one proviso for it to be rescinded, that of the locomotive failing a qualified engineer's examination, confirming that she was in good working order. I was also required to give an undertaking to effect payment by a bankers draft, if I was satisfied with her condition, and complete the purchase, by 3.00 p.m. on Friday 16 August, for a sum that was going to stretch my capabilities of raising funds to their limits, in the short time that had been stipulated. In 1968, money was not as readily accessible, the era of the plastic card, and the lottery had not yet arrived, an overdraft to a private individual, except to buy a house, would require the bank's lengthy investigation

before its decision - a probable refusal. Had I known of the almost insurmountable difficulties ahead, bearing in mind that for every £1 borrowed in 1968, one could expect to have to borrow in the order of £20 in 2008, readers will appreciate that I might very well have hesitated at this point in my endeavours!

Inspection of the locomotive was now obviously the first priority and 7.45 am on the Monday morning found me at Euston on a train for Preston. I completed the last part of my journey to Lostock Hall on a local bus which deposited me at my destination on a bridge overlooking the extensive sidings of the locomotive depot. The sight which greeted me, as I walked down the steep slope that led to the offices at the rear of the depot, would have saddened the most hardened of those remotely interested in railways and our industrial heritage; lines of various classes of locomotive which had been taken out of service over the previous months were rusting away after their enforced retirement. However, No 45110 was not amongst them, she had been moved into the covered and more secure protection of the loco shed, by the good offices of a canny lifetime railwayman, Shedmaster, Harold Sedgebeer, who greeted me on arrival. After the mandatory mug of sweet oily, ash-based tea, we threaded our way across the shed tracks between the lines of now silent locomotives. I recall clearly that short walk, under foot the ground was thick with a mixture of oil and ash, with water lying in puddles where ever you trod, and my first sight of Fiftyone-ten, her smart appearance, still bearing traces of the effort put in for the last day, and again before my arrival, enabling her to stand out against the forlorn lines of once fine locomotives, made all the more depressing by the dismal, damp and gloomy atmosphere, and uncanny silence of this recently bustling

depot, Harold earnestly described in his own words "She's one of the finest of the five's on shed, ne'er a candidate for the breakers yard and the office have told me I'm to tell you you've got 'till three on Friday" - THAT WAS THE MOMENT, I realised - forty years on, that is still etched in my memory, excitement and relief, that a reprieve had been officially granted, followed by the realisation of what lay ahead, initially in the next five days, and in the future, as I stood on the floor of the shed, looking up at the sheer mass of Fiftyone-Ten, all 127 tons of her. Harold could not, however, comprehend private individuals owning steam locomotives, and made considerable effort to elaborate on the pitfalls of maintaining a 'Black Five'. His words fell on deaf ears, but his thoughts were being expressed with the best of intentions; later when he realised my determination could not be influenced, he became a great supporter giving every possible assistance. What an asset he would turn out to be, in his final months before retirement whilst the locomotive was in his care.

Harold Sedgebeer now made arrangements for Fiftyone-ten to be moved by a diesel shunter into the morning sunshine, two locomotives, I recall blocking her path were drawn out and repositioned on the adjacent track as she emerged hauled by the shunter into the light. The comparison with all the decaying hulks that surrounded her is impossible to describe, and can probably only best be summed up in my personal thoughts. "I must not fail her in the important opportunity I had been given, I would save her, by some means or another, she was a excellent example of her class, and had achieved a place in railway history that must be acknowledged by permanent preservation, there could also be no more appropriate locomotive to fulfil the other important purpose in my saving her. Fiftyone-ten belonging to a class whose only four previously named examples had military connections, she was therefore ideally suited to bear the historically important name 'R.A.F. Biggin Hill" to acknowledge the legendary Kentish Battle of Britain airfield, located on one of the highest points of the North Downs overlooking London, from where in 1940, between 10 July and 31 October the Pilots and Ground Crew heroically won, at great loss of life the decisive air battles that were to be the turning point in our eventual victory in World War II. The previously an unnamed locomotive, No 45110 was an ideal candidate to replace my earlier unsuccessful efforts to save the former Southern Railway, Battle of Britain, class 4-6-2 No 34057 Biggin Hill; which through a confusion in locomotive numbers by BR's admin staff - all name plates having been removed in her last months of service - had been sold for scrap. In the early days of preservation, even when a locomotive was reasonably complete, recovery from a scrap yard was not generally considered an option at that time. There was no doubt in my mind, and in those who wrote to me later, that No 45110 would adequately fulfil two leading roles: First

Left **Lostock Hall:** The last day! Hardly believing this is the end, enthusiasts come to worship at Lostock Hall shed on 4 August 1968. Specially prepared, brightly polished 45110 and 70013 Oliver Cromwell stand in the yard ready to receive due devotions. *MJS*

Above **Grosmont (NYMR):** On 2 October 2005 Preserved Stanier 'Black 5' No 45110 re-enacts her historic role of heading British Rail's last main line steam hauled

passenger train into Liverpool Lime Street on 11 August 1968 which, it was thought at the time, would bring to an end the evocative era begun in 1825 of steam hauled trains on Britain's Railways. To mark the occasion No 45110 carries the now famous train reporting headboard 1T57 allocated to her on 11 August 1968. Awaiting arrival of her train and as she prepares to leave for Pickering *(Right)* as pilot to preserved Class mate No 45212. *Both D.Porter (Stafodex)*

45110
One of the few

in continuing to commemorate the historical importance she had just attained, in hauling the last steam train of BR; and second, in bearing the name *R.A.F. Biggin Hill* from where aircraft took part in the *Battle of Britain* one of the greatest battles in modem British history. A battle, much of which I had personally witnessed as a young man, and the airfield where I was later to be stationed in the Royal Air Force.

The race against time - is on....

In comparison to the other locomotives in the depot, even to my inexperienced eye, I could see she was in very good condition, the fitters also assured me they considered her to be in "fine fettle", my mind was made up, "I WOULD SAVE THIS LOCOMOTIVE". Harold Sedgebeer phoned BR's Preston office with my decision, and I left to sign the required paperwork, arriving there eventually with just over an hour to spare, I had met the first deadline. The next day after a night at a local boarding house, run by a retired railwayman and his wife who plied me with his war time experiences as a fireman and later as a driver of 'Black Fives', stories that would have made fascinating reading of the tenacity and bravery shown by train crews in war time.

I was at the sheds at 7.30 am on the Tuesday morning, but I had been preceded by an old family friend, a retired Shedmaster from Gateshead, Harry Tumbull, who having travelled down from Newcastle overnight was hard at work, a devoted supporter of steam locomotive preservation, whom I had contacted the previous evening to ask if he would, with his life long experience on locomotives carry out a detailed examination of No 45110 He agreed without hesitation. At about 10.30 am he emerged through the firebox door and with a 'thumbs up' gesture, confirmed my layman's opinion, professionally declaring the locomotive in good order. My lasting memory of that Tuesday morning will be Harry Turnbull whose head kept appearing, well blackened from the innermost depths of the locomotive, confirming, in his broad Geordie accent, his satisfaction with every mechanical or structural aspect which was greeted by Harold Sedgebeer, who spent his time walking up and down the length of the locomotive, turning to me from time to time, with the comment, "I told y'er so, I told y'er". I was in the company of two professional Railwaymen, whose banter was indecipherable, but whose knowledge was unquestionable. The real race to save No 45110 was now on, and

I confidently left for London by mid-afternoon, to raise the additional capital I required. Time was not on my side but I had not anticipated any great problems.

Tunnel vision and bureaucracy....

My requests for financial assistance to three of my local High Street Banks on the Wednesday morning was greeted either as a joke or an irritating waste of time, a motor car or washing machine, yes, a locomotive, NO! However one Manager aware of my determination suggested I visit their Head Office in the City, which I did later that afternoon in the firm belief they would receive my proposals more favourably. As I soon discovered Bankers in the City of London were not as accustomed, in the late sixties, to receiving unusual requests from private individuals as they might be today, and my request was completely beyond their comprehension: "Preserve a steam locomotive, what a bizarre idea". I would probably have done better if I had been a South American railway entrepreneur planning to build a railway through the Brazilian rainforests with a coach party of senior citizens, equipped with a pair of pruning shears! Thirty years on, how short sighted they were. As heritage, steam railways are now a principal recreational activity in this country with a multi-million pound turnover.

With time before BR's deadline now rapidly expiring, I spoke that evening with a number of friends with financial contacts In London. Eventually, through the good offices of a personal friend, I was put in telephone contact with a Director of one of our principal finance houses, to whom I again set out my proposals for the urgent need for funds to secure the locomotive. It was now 10.00 pm but at last I had a sympathetic ear, being ex RAF and having flown from Biggin Hill during the war, and as luck would have it, also with a keen interest in railways, he supported my efforts and confirmed he would give instructions in the morning for a loan to be reconsidered, The die however was not yet finally cast; bureaucrats in the bank at high street level on the Thursday morning kept raising the stakes on personal securities required, in addition to the funds I was providing, probably to placate their original attitude, and further precious time slipped away; but I refused to give up in my efforts to meet all

Below left **Minehead:** This is one of the rare breed of locomotives that were in steam right up to the last day and that managed to escape the cutters torch! 'Black 5' No 45110, on loan from The Severn Valley Railway, is seen here at Minehead on 16 March 2008 during the West Somerset Railway's Spring Gala. One week later she was back on SVR metals for the re-opening of the line following the floods of Summer 2007. *MJS*

Below **Bolton** 40 years ago in March 1968 Ray Ruffell captured No 45110 in steam at Bolton shed preparing to leave for its next tour of duty.

their preconditions to save No 45110 By 3.30 pm. I had met all their demands, I was to meet their Preston Branch Manager at 10.30 on Friday morning to inspect the locomotive, and if he was satisfied it existed, his branch would issue the draft. Tiredness was now taking its toll and I could not consider an overnight drive back to Preston, fortunately a 6.00 am departure from Euston would enable me to keep the appointment. To my relief the Manager was an ardent railway enthusiast and he endeavoured to contain his enthusiasm, when we arrived at Lostock Hall as he established the existence, if any were required, of the locomotive, while Harold Sedgebeer looked on shaking his head from side to side, muttering "get on with it man, get on with it." I concluded white collar Bank Managers and Shedmasters don't mix, the hostility was obvious.

With just over two and a half hours to go before BR's deadline expired and the scrap merchant, having now deposited his papers which included No 45110 I returned to the bank to collect the draft. There was yet to be another unbelievable delay, the bank's own

cheque book had been mislaid and twenty further precious minutes were lost while it was traced. It would probably have taken beyond the deadline to obtain a new book from another branch and this would have been too precipitous a situation to endure. At 12.55 pm I left the bank in a taxi and fifteen minutes later I handed the draft over to BR. In return, I received an insignificant consignment receipt, acknowledging the transfer of ownership and payment, in red ink, for: "Quantity: One. Steam Locomotive, viz: 'Class 5MT. No 45110'. (Dead on Wheels)". I was also passed a bundle of oil-stained sheets of paper, the result of years of handling in the repair workshops and her various depots, but there was a vital heading to each sheet, a group of stencilled numerals - 45110 - I now had the locomotive's essential paperwork, the vital current boiler certificate and maintenance records; and I had achieved my first goal:

THE LOCOMOTIVE WAS SAVED AND A SECURE FUTURE LAY AHEAD!

My ambitions to commemorate the legendary name of 'RAF Biggin Hill' complete, a few years later I had great satisfaction, tinged with some sadness, to pass ownership to the Severn Valley Railway and secure her future. The Severn Valley Railway, of which I have been privileged to be a director during its formative years, will be focusing on the 40th Anniversary re-run of IT57 with No 45110 heading a special train on 10 August 2008. However, for No 45110 it will be a more poignant affair as she requires a heavy overhaul having travelled many thousands of miles as a preserved locomotive. The Severn Valley Railway will mark this occasion by

ceremoniously dropping her fire on 11 August 2008 – the very same date forty years ago that I was making those frantic phone calls to save her from destruction.

No 45110 *R.A.F. Biggin Hill* has been based on The Severn Valley since 1971 and was present at Bridgnorth Station for the 30th Anniversary of the end of steam on 11 August 1998. Her boiler certificate has been extended to enable her to be present and hopefully in steam on the occasion of the 40th Anniversary on 11 August 2008. At the time of writing No 45110 is expected to enter a period of static display in The Engine House - the Severn Valley Railway's superb new visitor and education centre at Highley. Full details can be found on their web site at : http://www.svr.co.uk/

Below **Buxton:** There are trainspotters on every conceivable vantage point as the end draws near. Two 'Black 5' 4-6-0s carry out shunting duties under the watchful eye of the Signalman and his fine signal gantry during the last month of steam - very much a case of catch them while you still can!

LOCOMOTIVES WITHDRAWN AT THE END in 1968 and preserved		
Number	Status	Home base as at March 2008
43106	Under overhaul	The Severn Valley Railway
44806	In Service	The Llangollen Railway
44871	Under Restoration	The East Lancashire Railway
45025	Under Overhaul	The Strathspey Railway
45110	In Service*	The Severn Valley Railway
45212	In Service	The North York Moors Railway
45231	Under Repair	The East Lancashire Railway
45305	Under Repair	The Great Central Railway
48151	In Service Main Line	
48305	In Service	The Great Central Railway
48773	In Service	The Severn Valley Railway
70013	Under overhaul	The Great Central Railway
73050	In Service	The Nene Valley Railway
75027	In Service	The Bluebell Railway
92212	In Service	Mid-Hants Railway

Until Midnight on 11 August 2008 the 40th Anniversary of this locos haulage of the 15 Guinea Special last train

Lostock Hall No 70013 *Oliver Cromwell* receiving some last minute care and attention at Lostock Hall on 4 August 1968. Last of the class in operation, she has obviously been on the receiving end of much TLC of late and makes for a fine sight against the lack of care so vividly demonstrated elsewhere on the system.

One of 55 'Britannias' built by BR, *Oliver Cromwell* was built at Crewe Works, being completed on 30 May 1951. Initially allocated to Norwich Crown Point depot, she remained there until 1961 with the exception of a three month period at Stratford. A move to March came on 16 September 1961 before moving on to BR(MR) and Carlisle (Kingmoor) shed on 7 December 1963. During her stay in Carlisle, including a 21-month stint at Upperby shed, she entered Crewe Works on 3 October 1967 and became the last BR-owned steam locomotive to undergo routine heavy overhaul. The final allocation was to Carnforth on 6 January 1968, as the last of the Class. She was chosen to operate several specials at the death, culminating in the Fifteen Guinea Special of 11 August that year.

Following official withdrawal on 7 September, she was earmarked for the National Railway Museum's National Collection, replacing BR standard Class 7 4-6-2 No 70000 *Britannia* (which was later preserved privately), and despite a steam ban after the 11 August 1968, moved under her own steam on 12 August to her old shed at Norwich, and then on 13 August to Diss where she was transported to Bressingham Steam & Gardens. At Bressingham, she was in service to provide footplate rides until the 1980s, before retiring into the museum exhibition.

In 2004, she was selected for restoration back to main line standard and to be overhauled at the Great Central Railway with a view to hauling trains both on the Great Central and specials on the main line during 2008, to fittingly celebrate the passage of forty years, and the ongoing survival of steam motive power in the UK. *MJS*

The train crews on duty for *The Fifteen Guinea Special*

• Liverpool to Manchester Victoria
Locomotive No: 45110†
Driver: John Hart of Edge Hill Depot
Fireman: Brian Bradley
Guard: Henry Crossland of Edge Hill (working Liverpool to Blackburn)

• Manchester Victoria to Blackburn
Locomotive No: 70013 *Oliver Cromwell*
Driver: Harold Bolton **Fireman:** Tommy Gorman of Lostock Hall Depot

• Blackburn to Carlisle
Locomotive No: 70013 *Oliver Cromwell*
Driver: Robert Grogan of Blackburn Rose Grove Depot
Fireman: Raymond Watton
Guard: John Weal of Blackburn (working Blackburn to Carlisle arid back)

• Carlisle to Blackburn
Locomotive No: 44871
Driver: Norman Ashton of Blackburn Rose Grove Depot
Fireman: Anthony Helm,
Locomotive No:. 44781
Driver: Raymond Grimshaw **Fireman:** David Greenhalgh

• Blackburn to Manchester
Locomotive No: 44871
Driver: Edward Fothergill of Carnforth Depot
Fireman: John Thistlewaite *
Locomotive No: 44781
Driver: John Simpson **Fireman:** Ian Thistlewaite*

• Manchester to Liverpool
Locomotive No: 45110
Driver: Fred Smith of Edge Hill Depot
Fireman: Stephen Roberts
Guard: William Boardman of Edge Hill (working Blackburn to Liverpool)

• In charge of Locomotive Running:
HQ Locomotive Inspector: John Hughes
Catering Staff: Area Manager: F. Mann
Conductors: R. D. Maker and F. Birchall

* Brothers
† LMR Divisional Manager Richard Hardy also on the footplate

The Beeching Report (Part 1) published in 1963 entitled *The Reshaping of British Railways* had been met with shock and disbelief in many quarters. The press and media had of course had a field day. The planned closure of so many rural branch lines made emotive reporting easy to come by, but the loss of route mileage was only part of the picture. The following extract from the 1963 report is a summary of the cost savings expected:

THE FINANCIAL CONSEQUENCES OF THE PLAN

A summary, in broad terms, of the improvements in the working results of British Railways which it is estimated will result from the measures and proposals described in the plan is given below. Some of the savings would be more direct, immediate, and calculable, than others, but where ranges are shown they give a rough indication of the measure of uncertainty. To a large degree, proposals included in the plan are interdependent.
Condensation of the system, elimination of uneconomic services and traffics, reduction in rolling stock, through train working at the expense of wagon forwarding, the build-up of traffic on the main route network, and reduction of administrative expenses, are all closely linked. Therefore, realisation of many of the savings depends upon adoption of the plan as a whole. If the plan is implemented with vigour, however, much (though not necessarily all) of the Railways' deficit should be eliminated by 1970.

It is also important to realise that the elimination of cost factors will exceed the net savings expected from the various changes, and this will reduce the vulnerability of the Railways to further cost increases. At present, increases in the costs associated with the large volume of hopelessly unremunerative activities progressively undermine the potentially good railway services.

These estimates are not fully additive but are not subject to any serious measure of overlap. The list is not an exhaustive summary of the measures referred to in the body of the Report. In particular, whilst some of the estimates reflect improvements in efficiency associated with major changes, no figure is included to cover the summation of a multiplicity of efficiency improvements of a more detailed kind, which could be made with or without the plan. At this time, and in the face of great change, it would be unrealistic to formulate such an estimate, but there can be no doubt that higher standards of utilisation of staff and equipment will bring substantial rewards.
The proposals in respect of the continued replacement of steam by diesel traction, the introduction of Liner Trains, and the reorganisation of the arrangements for Sundries traffic, would involve capital expenditure of the order of £250m. There would, therefore, be a substantial rise in interest charges to set against the estimated financial improvement credited to these proposals. In addition to the proposals referred to in the plan, major modernisation works are already in hand, including

the electrification on the London Midland Region. These modernisation works will themselves contribute to the improvement in the financial position of British Railways.

	Estimated financial improvement of the order of £ m. per annum
Discontinuance and rationalisation of stopping passenger services and closure of stations to passenger traffic (after allowing for loss of contributory revenue)	18
Subsequent closure of lines and reduction from passenger to freight standard of maintenance of other lines following the withdrawal of services and closure of stations	11-13
Discontinuance of local freight services and closure of stations to freight traffic (after allowing for the preservation of potentially good traffics by alternative arrangements)	5-10
Direct savings arising from closures	34.41
Reduction in the fleet of gangwayed passenger coaches by the withdrawal of the stock reserved for peak traffics (after allowing for some loss of earnings)	2-3
Reduction in the fleet of wagons	10-12
Rationalisation of workshops—reduction in standing charges (apart from the effect of the fall in work load)	4
Continued conversion of steam to diesel traction	15-20
Reduction in the expenses of working coal traffic by— (a) the establishment of coal concentration depots in collaboration with the National Coal Board and the distributors, and (b) increased movement of coal in block train loads following the provision of train loading facilities at collieries	7-10
Concentration of sundries traffic	15-20
Introduction and development of Liner Trains—net earnings in five years time, say	10-12
Reduction in the loss on existing unprofitable traffics by commercial measures, say,	5-6
Additional net earnings assuming that traffic not on rail but which on several screenings, including cost screening, is seen to be favourable to rail, is secured to the extent of half the potential volume in the next five years; say,	10-15
Reduction in the expenses of general administration	3-4

This extract also provides a clear indication of the direction in which the contraction of the railway was planned to take over the coming years. Thus it can be seen that the emphasis was very much on reduction and cost saving, rather than on transport integration, infrastructure utilisation, redirection, expansion and promotion.

The Beeching Report (Part 2) published in 1965 was entitled *The Development of the Major Trunk Routes.*

Opposite page **Basingstoke Shed:** Seen through a glass darkly, 73018 and 80152 are most definitely endangered species as seen at Basingstoke on 2 July 1967, just a week from the end. Officially long closed, the shed building has obviously seen better days and one must presume that the broken panes have not occurred by accident.

Although still open for routine servicing of locomotives, staffing was minimal and certainly no deterrent to any potential vandal! New on 6 October 1951 and 17 November 1956, from Guildford and Eastleigh respectively, they both survived to the very end of steam on the SR one week on from this view. *MJS*

Appendix
'Endangered Species'

The end of steam across the length and breadth of Britain during the period covered by this book was probably one of the most visible public manifestations of change on the railway industry, but it was merely representative of a considerably greater effect that was gathering pace and would be set to last for many years to come as contraction was to be the order of things.

In the following pages we take a look back at a representative selection of some of the areas of the railway that would be effected by the contraction outlined in the Beeching Report.

We start with a piece from a man born into a 'railway family' as was the case with many railway workers...

DEMISE OF STEAM *The Practical View*

by Geoff Body 2008

I grew up with steam power. One grandfather was in charge of an agricultural steam engine and the other's farm provided the annual harvest excitement of the arrival of the thrashing machine rig led by an immaculate traction engine. Dad joined the Great Northern Railway starting work at Little Bytham on the GN Main Line while still in his teens, and I went straight from grammar school to the LNER at St Neots in 1945. This was hardly surprising as I was taken as a 6-year old to share the excitement of the first public run of Silver Link and a little later got my first invitation onto the footplate in the quiet backwater of Stamford East station. Steam reigned supreme and unchallenged in fact and in my subsconscious until the 1955 Modernisation Plan cast the first shadows of real change. It heralded the railbus and the dmu, which came to oust a host of small tanks and six-coupled branch line stalwarts and give substance to earlier experiments with diesel engined

railcars and shunters. Even more dramatic changes lay ahead with the rail network shrinking, high-capacity wagons and trainload working for freight and a sequence of electrification plans for the West Coast Main Line and busy commuter routes. As dedicated railwaymen we wanted all this despite a few grumbles along the way. After all it meant a real chance of survival and pride in our services.

My period at March Loco during Traffic Apprentice training brought the contrasting experiences of building a brick arch and firing on one of the elegant V2s working north to York and Newcastle. Mixed steam and diesel during a spell at Clacton for the summer season began to show the advantages of the latter and by the time we introduced the electric services on the Tilbury line the contrast was even clearer. Plaistow Loco did a magnificent job in keeping the last steam engines running but they were old and tired and money could not be wasted on long term repairs. The new electric trains gave both staff and passengers hope of a better future. At nearby Liverpool Street the GE section had teething troubles with the initial dual-voltage electrification while the 'Britannias' were impressing everyone on the Norwich services but even there steam was dying.

When the axe finally fell and steam locomotives disappeared from BR it seemed as if we had lost a slice of our history and in return had been provided with diesel traction which appealed to our professional need to go forward but was part of a whole trend towards depersonalisation and loss of character. Certainly the growing preservation movement was to offer hopes of compensation which it has, indeed, done so well, but a few days in Bold Colliery while steam locomotives accumulated for Rocket 150 celebrations at Rainhill really brought home to me what had been lost.

And so to the 'endangered species'...

Right **Leicester:** The extensive goods yards at Leicester (South) captured on 19 June 1962 as the 17.20 Nottingham (Victoria) to Marylebone, behind 'Royal Scot' Class 4-6-0 No 46163 *Civil Service Rifleman,* passes through on the main line. *Frank Cassell*

Below right **Clapham:** The steam carriage sidings at Clapham Junction extended to over 50 storage roads and are seen below on 3 January 1966 with 'Standard' Class 5, 4-6-0 No 73089 *Maid of Astolat* backing down to collect its next rake of carriages. This loco would be withdrawn at the end of September 1966 and sent for scrapping the following June. Sadly in this view she is already bereft of her name plate and not looking of her best - no way for a fair maiden to be seen let alone to show her name!

ENDANGERED JOBS
THE SHUNTER
THE END OF STEAM

Below: The shunter, with his pole, used to 'tie down' brakes and sheeting etc., would become an increasingly rare sight as the yards began to disappear. Note how smartly turned out he is complete with pocket watch and chain.

Goods Yards: The need to trans-ship goods between rail and road to provide effective delivery from door to door was cited as a major shortfall of freight by rail.

How short sighted was this view?

In 2008 the short or long wheel base van collects from the business door, travels to a central depot in the nearest large town - 'the hub' where it is unloaded and the parcels/goods reloaded on to massive articulated lorries. Often known as 'trunkers' these vehicles then travel between major towns and their respective 'hubs'. On arrival the parcels/goods are redistributed on to the short or long wheel base vans for delivery to the business door.

All seems rather familiar!

Hindsight is of course a marvellous thing and particularly in these ecologically more sensitive times, it can now be realised that a key difference in the two systems is actually the number of diesel engines required to operate the two versions of the same basic system.

Suffice to say back in the 1960s the road lobby won the day. The railway goods yards became endangered species as the branch lines closed, the feeder services were lost, smaller yards often

Left **Wadebridge:** The passenger service to Wadebridge ended on 31 January 1967. Freight traffic lingered on longer than in many such rural towns. The last freight train to Bodmin Parkway left on 4 September 1978. On 1 July 1961 Wadebridge goods yard was very much alive and active with a freight arriving behind Class 'N' 2-6-0 No 31834 from Padstow. On the right is Class '0298' 2-4-0 No 30585 one of just 3 examples (as finally rebuilt) of these fondly remembered Beattie tanks to be taken into British Railways service. All three were based at Wadebridge for working the Wenford Bridge china clay trains and other local goods traffic. They outlived the original 82 other class members, scrapped by 1899, by well over 60 years. Two are preserved - Nos. 30585 and 30587. *Terry Gough*

closed relatively soon after the passenger service was lost and all too soon even the larger yards - like Leicester (South) - came under threat. The decline gathered pace as the Motorway Network grew, providing faster road haulage timings over ever longer distances. A seemingly complete lack of foresight meant that not only were the tracks ripped up, but the track beds were lost through the sale of large sections for return to agriculture or for building of houses or factories - ironically often bringing in the very source of the revenue that could have saved the lines on which they were built! In 2008 of course journey times by road are lengthening in line with the next queue or bottleneck!

Carriage Sidings: The 'discontinuance and rationalisation of stopping passenger services' mentioned in the table *(on Page 143)* inevitably spelled the end for large numbers of carriages across the network. This in turn would see the end for many of the carriage sidings - large areas of land given over to storing these vehicles when not required.

The steam locomotive by its very nature had a number of basic requirements to operate on a day to day basis - the depot in which to stable and prepare the locomotive, the water and coal to fuel the locomotive, the oil needed to lubricate the motion, fuel for the lamps, shovels and other ancillary tools that travelled with the locomotive and of course the manpower to provide this support structure. Then of course there were the locomotive crews - the drivers and firemen. In order to ensure that all this was in place a considerable number of additional elements were needed.

ENDANGERED STRUCTURE
CARRIAGE SIDINGS
THE END OF STEAM

Loco crews for example would require accommodation - working long distances meant that it was not possible for all footplate and train crews to return to their home depot each night, this meant that there were hostels provided up and down the country. The crews would be awoken from their slumbers by 'The Knocker up', often the youngest recruit to the locomotive department who would ride around on his bike knocking on the doors of the crews to ensure they arrived at the depot on time to take their rostered loco off shed.

The list of jobs at an average size depot was surprisingly long and the following is just a selection of the jobs present:

Job	Brief summary of duties	Job	Brief summary of duties
Shedmaster	The Boss	Toolman	Maintenance and provision
Fire Droppers	Self explanatory	Storeman	Procurement and issue
Coal Men	Self explanatory	Lampman	Maintenance of running/shed lamps
Smokeboxers	Mainenance of smokebox	Brickie	Maintenance of loco firebricks
Ash Loaders	Ash pit clearance & disposal	Fitters	Locomotive maintenance & running repairs
Shed Turner	Turntable operations	Boilersmiths	Maintenance of Loco boilers
Lighters Up	Loco fire lighter	Carpenters	Maintenance & repair
Boilerwashers	Self explanatory	ATC Man	Automatic train control maintenance
Tubers	Tube replacement and maintenance	Knocker Up	'Alarm call for crews'
Sandman	Maintenance of loco sandboxes		

The locomotives reaching their depots at the end of the working day required servicing ready for the next tour of duty, this in turn meant that waste ash from the firebox would need to be removed and disposed of efficiently.

Ash Pits: There were many glamorous facets of our railway system, but the production by steam locomotives of ash and clinker – the residue from the burning of coal – was most certainly not one of them! From the earliest times, it became a task for some of the railways' lowliest rank and file to hand shovel the offending material into wagons, for onwards despatch, before the depots became buried under the stuff! This time honoured fashion survived virtually unchanged on the ex-GWR and SR systems, but not only was it dirty, hazardous and uncomfortable, there evolved an increasing difficulty in recruiting sufficient staff to cope. Especially on the larger sheds, this became a real headache. Hand shovelling, as the term implies, meant the sheer physical manhandling of the two elements from the locomotive, from firebox and smokebox. The simplest route was to the hard standing alongside the loco, but this then meant more shovelling into waiting wagons. Not a productive routine. Being thus expensive and time consuming, requiring armies of labourers, the LMS sought to solve by mechanisation. They built large ferro-concrete towers, alongside equally tall coaling plants, which could accept up to 25 tons in a bunker, fed by small wagons being hoist up the outside of the tower. When full, the loads could then be discharged into standard sized wagons for dispersal.

The LNER, by comparison, tried an innovative approach, resorting to sunken roads alongside the pits, which meant that the unwanted refuse could be hoist straight into waiting wagons. However, not all were totally 'sunk', leading to a preliminary shovel into a wheelbarrow before hoisting this up onto a ramp alongside the waiting wagons. Another LNER innovation, was the 'wet ash pit'. The major advantage was the virtual elimination of dust – leading to cleaner engines – but the filth still had to be lifted out of the pits (filled with water, remember) and this was by crane grab. Effective, but not the most economical method.

So, the struggle continued until the end of steam on BR…..but continues today wherever the steam engine rests after work!

Below **South Blyth:** This shed tended to be the poor relation to its northern neighbour across the water, especially for enthusiasts in latter days, as the fare on offer was less appetising. Staple of the shed for many years was Worsdell's 0-6-0s introduced in 1906 and classified as 'J27' by the LNER. One of the earlier built of the 115 members of the class, No 65813, stands on the South shed on 1 July, looking cold and unwanted and, indeed, this may have been the case, as it was officially withdrawn two weeks later and may have already been dispensed with on a day-to-day basis by the shedmaster. Coming to South shed on 27 March 1965, it had previously served BR at Percy Main shed without break and only left that location when the shed closed to steam on 28 February 1965. *MJS*

ENDANGERED STRUCTURE
STEAM LOCOSHEDS
THE END OF STEAM

Right **Guildford:** The scene at Guildford in the closing days of steam on the SR is very different! The shed staff will need to begin work soon on clearing this, before many more locos dump their waste here. In the part of Guildford shed yard adjacent to the station, 'Standard' Class 3 2-6-0 No 77014 stands in company with 'West Country Pacific' Class 4-6-2 No 34040 *Crewkerne*

Below **Lostock Hall:** As anyone who has 'enjoyed' a coal fire will

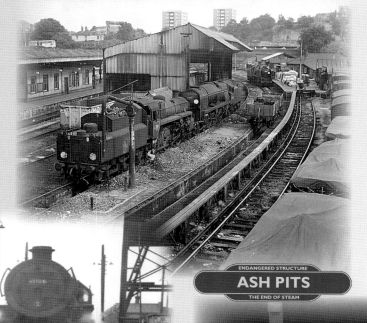

Below **Reading (Southern) Shed:** A job well done! Clearing the ash pit was a satisfying one but only at the last shovel full perhaps?

Bottom **Sunderland:** Another favourite design for sheds was the roundhouse. Employed from the earliest days, the design was a way of housing as many locomotives as possible under one roof in as small an overall area as possible. One advantage was that locos did not have to be shuffled around to escape from behind others, but the big drawback to roundhouses was if a turntable failed, or a loco failed on it! This is part of the example at Sunderland, seen on 1 July 1967, with Nos. 65855, 65811 and 65894 enjoying more sunshine. *MJS*

ENDANGERED STRUCTURE
ASH PITS
THE END OF STEAM

know, burning the fuel leads to deposits of ash being left behind On a steam railway, the problem was magnified! Ash pits were often constructed to accept the discharge of the unwanted material until a final disposal could be organised and there were varying types designed to cope with the problem, some restricted to specific regions and others limited to the largest sheds, where a greater throughout of locomotives obviously led to a magnified difficulty. Millions of tons thus recovered are probably now supporting countless thousands of buildings on landfill!. They were often dirty and uncomfortable places to work – see p.9 on the ex-GWR route, where hand shovelling out of the loco and away from the lineside survived until the end – especially if there had been rain and drainage from the pit was not all that it might be. The LMS, in contrast, moved to mechanisation through tall concrete towers, leading to such

as this view of the excavation under Class '4' 2-6-0 No 43106, in Lostock Hall yard on 23 March 1968, where the area is unusually clean although damp under the loco. '8F' Class 2-8-0 No 48727 stands to the left awaiting permission to move.

ENDANGERED STRUCTURE
ROUNDHOUSES
THE END OF STEAM

Water Cranes & Troughs: Water also needed to be made available and delivered to the tender/tanks. The volume required was considerable and obviously needed to be delivered as quickly as possible. This meant provision of mains supply and/or large water tanks and cranes to dispense it. The cranes were to be found on platform ends, at locosheds and in yards and carriage sidings. They came in a wide variety of forms and varied from region to region. Supply of water to the cranes was normally from tanks

fed by rainwater, streams and rivers or from mains supply. Water tanks were distinctive features in their own right and ranged in size, the largest would feed several cranes and the smallest would be a single crane and tank combined.

Such facilities were supplemented by water troughs at strategic locations on main lines where locomotives could pick up water at speed. The troughs were located in the centre of the tracks and a pick up scoop was carefully lowered from under the tender to dip into the water and the train's forward momentum forced gallons of water into the tank over a very short distance. Crews had to be very attentive during this process ensuring the lowering and raising of the scoop was carried out at precisely the right times.

WATER CRANES
ENDANGERED STRUCTURE — THE END OF STEAM

Top left **Woking:** Driver Anderson of Nine Elms turns the wheel as his fireman watches the cascade into the tender. Meanwhile, 'West Country' Class 4-6-2 No 34098 *Templecombe* quietly pollutes the atmosphere at Woking on 15 January 1967, pausing with a 9.33 a.m. Waterloo - Bournemouth excursion.

Top right **Machynlleth:** A slightly different arrangement was that seen at Machynlleth on 12 July 1966, where the pipe to the loco came direct from the water tower, rather than up through the column. Also, the fireman here is having to do everything himself!

Above **Lostock Hall:** As well as platform ends, loco sheds, were places vital for replenishment. On 23 March 1968, '8f' Class 2-8-0 No 48132 receives a drink before going off shed for her next duty.

Right **Brock:** Water is a vital ingredient for steam locomotives but constantly having to stop to replenish emptying tanks was at best an irritation and at worst a potential disaster and disruption to other services. One solution employed by many railways was the provision of water troughs, Brocks Troughs were situated just north of Brock station and south of the junction for the Knott End branch from Garstang in Lancashire. In a view from around 1937, LMS 'Black 5' 4-6-0 No 5058 is running over the troughs with a special with a rich mixture of stock, including a bullion van next to the engine and horse boxes! *MJS collection*

WATER TROUGHS
ENDANGERED STRUCTURE — THE END OF STEAM

Turntables: Locomotive haulage of trains had been the modus operandi since the earliest days of the railway and primarily the steam locomotive, particularly the tender locomotive, was built to travel in one direction. Although they could run tender first this was restricted due to visibility, speed and safety.

Unlike the diesels and electrics that would replace them the steam locomotive required a means to turn them round to enable them to operate in the correct direction for the rostered service. To enable this to happen turntables were made available throughout the system. These were of varying designs and sizes, operation also varied from simple man power to the luxury of vacuum operation utilising the engines steam power via the vacuum brake pipes.

ENDANGERED STRUCTURE
TURNTABLES
THE END OF STEAM

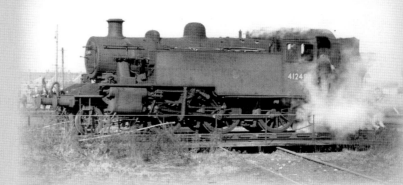

Left **Guildford:** The table at Guildford forms an integral part of the shed design, squeezed into the hillside with a half-roundhouse and the table controlling inwards and outwards movements of the shed. A more substantial table than some, complete with a corrugated iron shelter for the operator, this sees 'Standard' Class 5 No 73118 *King Leodegrance* being turned at the end of the day on 16 February 1967.

Below **Rose Grove:** Whilst operating on the basic premise, of enabling a locomotive to be turned through any part of 360°,

the designs and choices of locations could vary greatly. Out in the open shed yard, but alongside the shed wall, away from the main business, the turntable at Rose Grove plays host to '8F' Class 2-8-0 No 48666 which is making use of the vacuum pipe to power the table on 23 March 1968.

Above **Highbridge:** Even some small sheds had their own versions, which were often more 'flimsy' affairs to match the predominantly lighter engines expected to use them. On 5 March 1966, Class '2' 2-6-2T No 41249 uses Highbridge's.

Below **Heaton Mersey**: Keeping the locomotives running was of course vital - stopping them was probably even more important! As with the motor car, there are

ENDANGERED PARTS
BRAKE BLOCKS
THE END OF STEAM

ENDANGERED JOBS
THE SHEDMASTER
THE END OF STEAM

all manner of pieces to a steam engine that could fail or wear out sufficiently to need replacement. One such item – vital to both forms of transport – is brake blocks. It was not unusual to see piles of these items stacked up against a shed wall, as in this view of Heaton Mersey shed on 28 March 1965. Class '4' 2-6-0 No 43042 and '8F' Class 2-8-0 No 48273 enjoy the shafts of sunlight through another variation in shed roofs, this time with plenty of glass to brighten up the interior. These of course were not endangered to the extent of extinction but the piles were considerably smaller as the steam locomotives and surplus rolling stock disappeared. *MJS*

Right: The Shedmaster Rank was ever important on the railway and status could easily be judged by style of uniform – or even lack of! – and 'titfer'. The 'gaffer' stands for his portrait by one of his locos, complete with spit-polished shoes, waistcoat, raincoat and trilby, looking every inch the part. To the trainspotter here was often the man most feared! 'Bunking In' to sheds would garner the wrath, while on the other hand a polite request was often rewarded!

Main picture **Bolton:** Can this really be just 40 years ago? As we write this in April 2008 both your authors are experiencing those mixed feelings that an evocative shot like this can so often engender! On the one hand it seems like only yesterday, the cobbled streets, the back to back housing, the smell of coal, ash and anthracite. The brick

wall awaiting perhaps the next kick of the football, by perhaps the next budding Francis Lee - those impromptu back street football matches were so much easier then, often with not a car in sight! On the other hand it all seems so long ago, the smell of steam and the smokier atmosphere all but a distant memory!

The cheerful smile of Connie Ruffell as she crosses the street with Bolton shed as a backdrop, reminds us of the fun we had chasing those ever more illusive 'last of the few' locos and of the characters we met along the ash and cinder paths en-route to those 'Meccas' of steam!

Coaling stages: Coal had to be transported to the steam locomotive depots from the collieries, which of course was no great problem for an industry responsible for moving millions of tons of 'black gold' to fuel the nations domestic fires and industrial furnaces! This was achieved for the most part in long trains of loose coupled open wagons. These wagons were not air braked and when steeper down grades were encountered the train would be bought to a halt and the brakes would have to be applied on several if not all of the wagons to assist in train braking as it proceeded down the incline. Those readers interested in learning more can see preserved examples of mineral waggons at *The Great Central Railway, Loughborough, Leicestershire* - home to 'The Windcutter' a unique set of over 30 such waggons.

Once the coal arrived on site equipment was needed to load it into the locomotive bunkers and tenders, giving rise to massive mechanised coaling towers at large sheds, semi mechanical loaders at medium sized depots, down to hand barrowing and loading from simple staithes at small wayside sheds. The large coaling towers were dubbed The Cenotaph, any reader who has seen London's Cenotaph in will appreciate the comparison!

Above **Bolton:** The concrete tower at Bolton seen on 23 March 1968, with No 48026 nearby on the disposal pit.

Below **Lostock Hall:** On the same day, a similar design is at Lostock Hall, with another '8F' Class 2-8-0 , No 48132, being turned on the table.

FIREMEN

ENDANGERED JOBS
THE END OF STEAM

ENGINE DRIVERS

ENDANGERED JOBS
THE END OF STEAM

Above: The day's turn finished, locos Class '5' 4-6-0 No 44677 and 'Britannia' Class 4-6-2 No 70011 *Hotspur* 'put to bed', fireman and driver pose for the camera before signing off...

Below: **Hot and sweaty** it could be, or cold and draughty, but the opening of the fire doors could make for more discomfort in either case, making matters worse in the summer or only briefly alleviating the chill in the winter with a sudden blast of hot air. Add to the fact of needing agility and continued strength to lift the shovel from tender to firebox on a rocking footplate and it was not a job for the fainthearted. Skill and dexterity was required to accurately 'fire' the coal into the desired part of the loco's furnace. This is Fireman Brian Cobbett aboard 'Standard' Class '4', 2-6-0 No 76031 'putting a bit in the corners'.

WV.64

Main picture: Ray Ruffell was not a man to shy away from taking a photograph in more difficult conditions. Come rain or shine foul weather or fine he would most times have his camera at the ready. Working as a Guard on the Southern Region during the 1960s meant he was able to capture unusual shots like this one. Taken through the window of the driving compartment of an EMU running on the slow line, in the last few days of Southern Region steam. The Driver and fireman of 'Battle of Britain' Class 4-6-2 No 34060 25 *Squadron*, already bereft of the highly prized nameplate and squadron badge, the frame for which is clearly visible, are captured as they hurry past, overtaking on the fast line. Note the fireman's handkerchief hat, a popular form of headgear of years gone by, seen twice now within this book, but not so often seen in 2008!

Below: Seated, relaxed, hand on the throttle and eye on the road....

34060

ENDANGERED JOBS
FITTERS
THE END OF STEAM

Left **Eastleigh Shed:** 4 June 1967 and Class '4' 2-6-4T No 80016 is receiving some (presumably) much-needed 'emergency' attention, under the watchful eye of the loco's driver above. This loco was withdrawn just over a month later and languished at Eastleigh until November 1967 when it was despatched to Bird's breakers yard at Risca. Perhaps the 'emergency' attention was of a more terminal nature than the expressions in the picture would suggest?

Right **Guildford Shed:** *"No that's OK we can manage..."!* One can almost hear them saying it, probably under their breath, although the fitter next to the up-ended 'Q1' Class 0-6-0 No 33018 seems to be scratching his head in disbelief that his two colleagues are managing to roll the driving wheels towards the waiting locomotive. This was a 'hot

box' repair - worn bearings needing replacement - and as all the Q1s were withdrawn by the end of 1966 this would probably be the last repairs

carried out to this member of the Class. One 'Q1' survives No 33001 is part of the National Collection based at York Museum.

ENDANGERED JOBS
CLEANERS
THE END OF STEAM

Left **Bolton:** Cleaning a large loco is a long job and even more so as already seen in this view on *page 127*, from Bolton on 23 March 1968. Although he may have had due pride at the end, no doubt this young man could think of many things he would rather have been doing!

EXTINCT ROLLING STOCK
SLIP COACHES
THE END OF STEAM

Main Picture **Bicester North:** The very last slip coach used on British Railways, was detached from the back of the 5.10pm Ex-Paddington to Wolverhampton Express on 10 September 1960 and therefore falls just prior to the main period 1965-1968 under review within these

pages. However your authors felt the subject would be of sufficient interest to our readers to include this wonderful shot of a slip coach, on the very same service, but a few months earlier on 31 May 1960. Should our esteemed readers need further justification for inclusion the subject was noted in the response to a letter in the *Railway Magazine* of January 1965 *(see right)*.

The slip coach having just arrived in the centre road at Bicester North, 'Hall' Class 4-6-0 No 4907 *Broughton Hall* has coupled up and will set forward beyond the crossover before setting back into the platform where the Hall's own train the 4.34pm Paddington to Wolverhampton stopping service is waiting behind the photographer. The slip coach No W7071W will be attached to the front and will go forward as part of this service.

Slip coach working

LATTERLY, the release operation in slip carriage working was provided by a hinged coupling hook on the front of the slip portion of the train, normally held rigid by a sliding bar passing in front of it, but caused to drop when this bar was withdrawn by the action of a lever under the slip guard's control. An adaptor allowed the slip to take its heat from the train system, but separated and sealed itself automatically after the carriage had been dropped. Automatic sealing also took place after the slip in the train vacuum brake pipe, as otherwise the brakes would have been applied following the normal principle that a breakaway brings both portions of the train to a standstill. Although there were exceptions, corridor connections were not usually provided on slip coaches, which had a special guard's compartment at one end.

The slip guard was warned of where to operate the slip by means of small lineside signals. Before effecting the severance, he applied his hand-brake slightly to ensure that the slip would draw well behind the main train directly the former was detached. When running under its own momentum, the slip gave warning of its approach to men working on the line by a foot-operated bell. Where this momentum was not sufficient for the portion to attain the requisite station platform, a shunting locomotive would be attached after the main train had cleared the section. This occurred, for instance, at Heywood Road Junction, Westbury, where for many years the down "Cornish Riviera Express", routed via the cut-off, slipped its rear portion (for the Weymouth line), which had to be shunted into Westbury Station.

The Great Western Railway was the principal exponent of the once-numerous slip coach services in Great Britain and it was only on the Western Region of British Railways that they were reintroduced after the second world war. The last, the Bicester slip coach on the 17.10 train from Paddington, was withdrawn from the beginning of the winter timetables on September 12, 1960.

[Reply to J. G. BENSTEAD]

London Midland Region
Eastern Region
North Eastern Region
Scottish Region
Southern Region
Western Region

Right **Blue Anchor:** Who needed a hotel with, possibly, a long walk to the beach, when you could arrive by train and stay in a Camping Coach close to the station and right by the seaside? The beach chalets at the far end of this view of the two coaches at Blue Anchor exemplify the convenience of their location.
R M Casserley

ENDANGERED ROLLINGSTOCK
CAMPING COACHES
THE END OF STEAM

CAMPING COACH LOCATIONS	
A 1960s regional selection	
Abergele	Conwy
Bakewell	Derbyshire
Bassenthwaite	Cumbria
Betws-y-Coed	Conwy
Blackpool SG	Lancashire
Coniston	Cumbria
Corton	Suffolk
Felixstowe Pier	Suffolk
Hopton on Sea	Norfolk
Lowerstoft (N)	Suffolk
Mundesley	Norfolk
Oulton Broad (S)	Norfolk
Robin Hood's Bay	N. Yorkshire
Scalby	N. Yorkshire
Bolton Abbey	N. Yorkshire
Goathland	N. Yorkshire
Ravenscar	N. Yorkshire
Staithes	N. Yorkshire
Aberfeldy	Perthshire
Arisaig	Inverness-Shire
Benderloch	Argyle & Bute
Fortrose	Highland
Glenfinnan	Highland
Kingussie	Highland
Tyndrum Lower	Stirlingshire
Bere Ferrers	Devon
Corfe Castle	Dorset
East Budleigh	Devon
Wool	Dorset
Wrafton	Devon

Not everyone's idea of holiday accommodation. However those who experienced this rather 'alternative' type of holiday very often got bitten by the bug and returned year after year! First introduced way back in 1933 by the London & North Eastern Railway and quickly followed by the other 'big four' railway companies, the re-use of carriages, who's normal working life had come to an end, proved popular and provided an additional source of income. The carriages were for the most part converted and maintained in the railway company's own workshops thus providing additional work for the Carriage & Wagon Departments. The Camping Coaches were strategically sited at holiday destinations, often, but by no means always at or close to seaside resorts. In the days before the growth in the number of families owning a motor car the railways of course benefited further by the fact that many families would travel to the station at which the coaches were based, by train and the price structure was designed to encourage this. The carriages were looked after by the station staff as part of their overall duties, this included cleaning and preparing them for each new arrival and the day to day requirements of the paying guests. The fact that the carriages for the most part were parked on sidings still connected to the rail network meant that at the end of the season they could be hauled back to the workshops for refurbishment as required and delivered back in time for the following season. With the closure of many rural and seaside destination branch lines, during the late 1950s and throughout the 1960s, many of the Camping Coach locations were lost and as a result the numbers dwindled.

The *Railway Magazine* of February 1965 reported *Fewer camping coaches* available for the coming season a trend that was to continue for the next six years until the last bookings from the general public were taken by The London Midland Region of British Railways for the 1971 season. Just a few were retained to provide holiday accommodation for railway staff and their families. At the time of writing eight Camping Coaches survive at Dawlish Warren at *The Brunel Camping Coach Park* and are once again available for booking by the public at large.

Aberayron	Ceredigion
Aberdovey	Gwynedd
Blue Anchor	Somerset
Buckfastleigh	Devon
Fairbourne	Gwynedd
Gara Bridge	Devon
Lustleigh	Devon
Symonds Yat	Monmouth
Tintern	Monmouth

Fewer camping coaches
THERE will be fewer railway camping coach sites this year, and some of the older four- and eight-berth coaches are to be withdrawn. However, 58 sites in Southern England, on the East Coast and in North Wales and Scotland are to remain open, and more than 120 six-berth coaches, including Pullmans, will still be available for booking from March until September. There will be no camping sites at the North-East coastal resorts between Newbiggin-on-Sea, Northumberland, and Hornsea, Lincolnshire, and on the Western Region, in South Wales, Cornwall and Devon. Many of the sites abandoned were on branch lines now closed. Most of the withdrawn coaches are stated to be those on which maintenance at reasonable standards is proving uneconomic.

Index

Below **Devils Bridge:** So, steam on British Railways (or 'British Rail' as it had by then become!) ended on 4 August 1968? Not quite! The Vale of Rheidol Railway (VoR) is a 1 ft 11¾ in (603 mm) narrow gauge heritage railway that runs for 11¾ miles between Aberystwyth and Devil's Bridge in Wales. Quietly continuing its life as a tourist railway, unnoticed by many of those chasing their beloved steam locos around the northwest in the final days, it was the last line to be operated by steam as part of the nationalised British Railways network, until it was privatised in 1989. The locos had been inherited by the GWR in 1923 and by BR in 1948 and were still very active when the standard gauge steam finished in normal day-to-day duties. A couple of years earlier, on 20 July 1966, 2-6-2T No 7 *Owain Glyndŵr* has run round its train, having arrived at Devil's Bridge with the 1.30 p.m. from Aberystwyth and now receives a little attention prior to hauling the return working.

1968

Not quite the end of Steam on British Railways!

The prospect of a country without steam locomotives and railways on which to run them was by 1968 already a concept consigned to the scrap yard! In fact as far back as 1950 *The Talyllyn Railway Preservation Society* had been formed by enthusiasts to save the narrow gauge Talyllyn Railway from extinction. The first passenger trains under Preservation Society auspices ran at the Whitsun holiday of 1951.

Since those early days Heritage Railways have been developing nationwide and through sheer hard work grit and determination, impossible dreams have more often than not been turned into reality. No book on the end of steam or indeed on *Not quite the end of steam,* can end without reference to, and recognition of, the monumental contribution made by one man...

David Lloyd Victor Woodham was born in 1919 and having joined the family dock porterage business in Barry, South Wales, as a young man, he was destined to become known as ***Dai Woodham, the saviour of steam!*** Between 1959 and 1968 his company - Woodham Brothers of Barry purchased no fewer than 297 steam locomotives from British Railways for scrapping. Due to the constant flow of wagons for scrap and the fact they were easier to dispose of, the locomotives were 'kept for a rainy day'. Gradually over the years locomotives were reserved one by one, the final departure being No 5553 but not before 212 others had left the yards for preservation or to contribute parts to other projects. Dai Woodham sadly passed away on 12 September 1994 but he will surely be remembered for as long as a preserved steam locomotive turns a wheel!